Ken Gaub is my friend, and a man that lives and breathes what he speaks. Ken is an author and a speaker who has the ability to touch your life with humor, and your heart with love. You will see his gifting in this book. It will encourage you to be all you are in Christ.

> Pastor Ron Coleman
> Grace Church Ministry
> Chester, IL

This book is the culmination of a life totally committed to winning people to Christ. Dr. Ken Gaub gives valuable insights into wisely influencing others to follow the Lord. He has embodied these proven principles for almost 50 years of effective worldwide ministry in many of the world's greatest churches.

> Dr. Charles H. Gaulden
> Evangel Cathedral
> Spartanburg, SC

Go into all the world . . . Ken Gaub is doing this without any concern for himself. He is on a mission and that mission is souls for the kingdom. God has called every believing Christian to be a soul winner. This book tells you how to do it, regardless of the setting you're in. So begin to read, then meditate on how to lead your family, friends, and associates to Christ. I believe this book will help many of us in sharing the love of God with unbelievers.

> Duane Arneson
> Cornerstone Ministries
> Sioux Falls, SD

Ken Gaub is no theoretician . . . he is a practitioner with a lifelong career of motivating people. He knows how to make truth usable. I've watched him, listened to him, and read his books most of my life. Winning people to Christ is not about clever words or slick programs, it's simply knowing how to radiate the authentic life that's within you. Ken knows how to, and wants to encourage everyone to let God use them. You'll do well to listen.

> Phil Derstine
> Christian Retreat
> Bradenton, FL

Ken Gaub has a unique way of winning souls. I've been with him in Russia, all over the Middle East, and in Australia, and he always makes soul winning a priority. With his unusual wit and humor, he always reaches for an opportunity to win a person to Christ. Proverbs tells us that "he that winneth souls is wise." Ken Gaub is a wise man — he knows the value of a soul. This book will challenge your life.

> Bill Heaston
> Bridges of Love Ministry
> Lakeland, FL

Ken Gaub is a soul winner — passionate, persistent, and, most importantly, effective in communicating. I have constantly been challenged by his example to care more and try harder to win people. To Ken, soul winning is as natural as breathing. He's a great teacher on this subject, because he has honed his skills. His enthusiasm is contagious. I have always felt that if you want to learn something right, learn it from the best. Ken Gaub is the best soul winner I know.

> Cal Carpenter
> Senior Pastor, Sound Life Church
> Spanaway, WA

WHAT'S YOUR PASSION?

WHAT'S YOUR PASSION?

Proven Tips for Witnessing to
Anyone, Anytime, Anywhere

KEN GAUB

New Leaf Press

First printing: September 2004

Copyright © 2004 by Ken Gaub. All rights reserved. No part of this book may be used or reproduced in any manner whatsoever without written permission of the publisher, except in the case of brief quotations in articles and reviews. For information write: New Leaf Press, Inc., P.O. Box 726, Green Forest, AR 72638.

ISBN: 0-89221-589-5
Library of Congress Number: 2004106955

Cover by Left Coast Design, Portland, Oregon

Note: This book contains quotes by a number of people. The use of a quote does not mean a blanket endorsement of all their views or their lives by this author.

All Scripture references are from the King James Version unless otherwise noted.

Printed in the United States of America

Please visit our website for other great titles:
www.newleafpress.net

For information regarding author interviews, please contact the publicity department at (870) 438-5288.

I dedicate this book on soul winning to every person who has accepted Jesus Christ through this ministry.

I also dedicate it to my staff, without whose help this book would not have been possible.

But most of all I dedicate this book to Jesus.

If He had not given His life for us, and touched my life, this book would not have any point.

CONTENTS

FOREWORD

Ken Gaub is a delightful character, brilliant and dedicated to Christ. I have known Ken for almost 40 years. Each time I see him, even for a brief breakfast, I walk away thankful for new ideas he has shared with me about winning souls.

We laugh with each other. I've shared with Ken that when I talk to a reluctant person, my soul-winning line is this: "Give your heart to Jesus, try Him for six months. If you don't like how things are going, you can get all your sins back."

I'm going to try to remember every page of this new book. Ken leads more people to Jesus outside the church one-on-one than anyone I know.

Every pastor should buy cases of this new book.

Lowell Lundstrom
Pastor/Evangelist
Minneapolis, Minnesota

INTRODUCTION

I t's been in my heart for some time to release a book that people could use as a manual for winning people to Christ. But then I thought, *There are a lot books on the subject, and besides, I have another book coming out this year. I don't want people to just try to copy me. They each have their own personality and need to use it.*

But recently I really felt the Lord spoke to my heart to get the book done. I called Tim Dudley, Jim Fletcher, and Don Enz at New Leaf Press/Master Books, and they seemed excited. I also believe the Lord led me as to what to include.

As I talked to my pastor friends, many told me that this is a book that is needed now. One pastor said he wanted a thousand copies — another said he wanted five hundred. We know Jesus is coming soon, so we'd better do what we can while we can still do it.

Lowell Lundstrom, a great pastor/evangelist, keeps asking me, "When is that book coming out?" Well, here it is. . . .

In this book, we are going to talk about how to capture their attention, so they will start listening and stop ignoring.

God doesn't want us to just die and go to heaven. He thinks it would be a good idea if we would live and go to work for Him.

If awards happen in heaven, the staff of New Leaf Press/ Master Books will undoubtedly receive one for souls saved because they published this book.

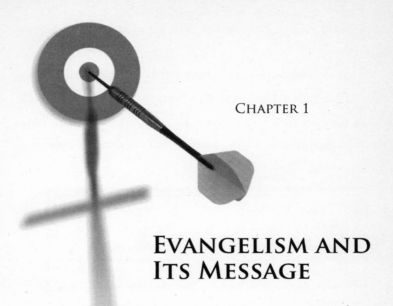

CHAPTER 1

EVANGELISM AND ITS MESSAGE

As we look around, we wonder, *Don't we have enough religions, churches, temples, synagogues and other places of worship?* Most people think so. It seems everyone has religion. It's not about being a Baptist, a Presbyterian, a Catholic, a Methodist, or a Pentecostal. A relationship with God is more than a building to worship in; it's more than just religion; it's a personal relationship with Jesus Christ as our Lord and Savior.

Winning the lost to Christ is my passion. I believe everyone needs a real, personal relationship with Jesus Christ. Jesus came to give life, not death; He died that we could live.

We don't have to go to college to learn how to sin. It's in our nature. We do this all by ourselves just like Adam and Eve. Our sin causes a break between us and God. We always want to do things our own way. That's what gets us into trouble.

If we don't accept Christ into our life, we become slaves to sin. When we believe what's wrong, we start to doubt what's right. A classic example is the story of Adam and Eve. Eve believed Satan's story, then began to doubt God. The rest is history.

> *For God so loved the world that he gave his only begotten son, that whosoever believeth in him should not perish, but have everlasting life.*
>
> John 3:16

Every time I visit Bethlehem, my heart beats a little faster, and tears come to my eyes. It was in Bethlehem over 2,000 years ago that God's gift of Jesus made His entrance onto this planet. He was and is today the Savior of the world, the Prince of Peace, the mighty God, the Counselor and the everlasting Father.

Jesus didn't come here for "religious" reasons, but that the world could be saved. We can turn over a new leaf, promise to do better, give money to the church or a charity. This is all good, but it's not what's truly important. First of all, we need a personal relationship with Jesus Christ!

"To all who received (Jesus) . . . he gave power to become children of God" (John 1:12;RSV). We are children of God when we receive Jesus as our savior. We don't become perfect because we become a Christian, but our nature is changed and we begin to strive for perfection. (1 John 2:1) Now you have the power (Phil. 4:13) to reach your area for Christ.

The Lord is not willing that any should perish. So what are we going to do about the *pre-Christians*? We need a real passion to win people to Christ and get them involved in this wonderful new family. This is called Kingdom vision.

I believe that this book will totally change the way Christians think and they will begin to lead people to Christ. The growth of a church can explode if people catch the vision.

I don't want to just preach great sermons to a nice-looking crowd of people. I want to touch hurting, messed-up people.

Yes, some of them are in the church, but a lot more don't even darken the door of any church. We don't want to miss these opportunities. It's time to wake up, put up, or shut up.

According to one survey by the Barna Institute, about 43 percent of American adults attend church on a typical weekend. This percentage has varied only a few points over the past 20 years, peaking in 1986 at 49 percent.

The top three reasons people give for attending a particular church are:

1. The doctrine and beliefs of that church.
2. How much the people seem to care about each other.
3. The quality of the sermons that are preached.

Those who call themselves Protestants are more likely to attend than are Catholics. Older people are more likely to attend than middle-aged, who in turn are more likely to go than younger adults. Attendance is also higher in the South and Midwest (the "Bible Belt") than in the Northeast and West.

Another item that is noteworthy is that adults who attended church regularly as children are three times as likely to be attending church today than those who did not attend as children. About seven out of ten of today's adults had a period of time as children when they did attend church or Sunday school, and well over half of those who attended as children take their own children. They are also more likely to pray to God during a typical week than those who did not attend church as children.

The message of evangelism is very important. It's our commission. Jesus told us to spread the gospel everywhere. It should also be our passion. It's not religion, as such. It's a lot more than that.

Who or what age should be our "target?" Here are some interesting statistics.

1. Children between the ages of 5 and 13 have a 32 percent probability of accepting Christ as their Savior. This drops to 4 percent for teens aged 14–18. For those over 18, the probability rises to 6 percent.

2. Only 4 percent of adults could accurately define the "Great Commission," quote John 3:16, and define "the gospel."

Who is most likely to share their faith? While 58 percent of born-again Christians claim to have shared their faith during the past year, Protestants from non-mainline churches are the most likely (63 percent), next come the mainline Protestants (52 percent), and Catholics (48 percent).

In this fast-paced, high-pressure life, the world and people are changing on a daily basis. People scoffed about man going to the moon. Now we have put robots on Mars, over three hundred million miles away, and we are starting to talk about putting men on Mars. But the gospel of Jesus Christ remains the same.

I have found in many churches that it's mainly the young people who have heard the voice of God. They carry the passion to win people to Christ. They seem to have evangelism on their minds. They are purpose- and passion-driven. They want to change their world. They

> *I want you to think*
>
> *outside the box.*

aren't ashamed to stand up for what is right. They will go out and talk to people about Jesus. They will do it everywhere — in the marketplace, the streets, their schools.

Many believers are being radically changed and are letting the Holy Spirit lead their lives. They are breaking out of their status quo, their comfort zone, and realizing what the Great Commission of "Go ye" is really all about.

> *Mark 16:15 says, "Go ye into all the world and preach the gospel to every creature."*

God has always used people — from the disciples forward — to implement His plan. He has used people without college degrees, and college professors with several degrees — football coaches, hippies, housewives, farmers, mechanics, sales people, and even Hollywood actors.

> How do we move forward to win the pre-Christians?

Most people are too busy with their own lives, building careers and making money. In general, they just don't make the time to touch others. It's one thing to be busy; it's another to be productive. Life in general is just too complicated and fast. I know my own life is so busy I have to take time daily to seek God and ask for direction. I don't mean just a short devotion; I'm talking about spending hours in prayer.

Jesus worked with His disciples. They watched Him. They were His witnesses. They saw and understood His vision and felt His passion. He told them His purpose. It states in John 20:30–31 that Jesus did a lot of things in front of His disciples that were not recorded. The things that were written were written that we might believe in Him. The first epistle of John assures us that John is passing on to us the truth, so that we might also have fellowship and full joy (1 John 1:1–4).

Jesus went about doing His mission and did not get sidetracked by the religious folks of the day. Some criticized and ridiculed Him. His vision was clear, His motives were pure.

It was always on His mind to redeem the world. He knew why He was here. He lived a "purpose-driven life."

His mansions were in Heaven and He was going there to prepare a place for us. This would be after He gave His life to save us. His life was committed to the ultimate purpose. Not for one second did he lose track of the goal. He did not waste any of His life or time or energy. He didn't give altar calls — didn't ask people to raise their hands or sign a card. He met people on their level and showed His concern. He loved them and set them free.

> *JESUS HAD NO BACK-UP PLAN —*
> *NO PLAN B.*

His plan would work. His plan would not fail. His real concern was not in a religious program, but to redeem the world. He enlisted men to help Him and carry on after He was gone.

Jesus was radical. He got to the root of problems. His lifestyle did not fit into the accepted scheme of His day.

Many of the men He enlisted grew up in the "back woods" around Galilee and some were easily offended. This motley crew of men He handpicked didn't seem to be the kind of men that could win the world. But Jesus saw them as potential leaders. Some of these men were ignorant, un-learned, without influence, and awkward, but fed up with the hypocrisy of religion. However, they were teachable and pliable in the hands of the Master with a plan and purpose.

Jesus was interested in quality, not just quantity. We were all born to reproduce. I've seen some churches claiming hundreds and even thousands are getting saved, but the church shows no real growth. We need to see honest results.

> *Just think what the Lord could do with and through us, if we really understood His purpose, and what He has in store for us.*

It's one thing to have people answer an altar call, it's another to truly disciple them. God knows the truth, He is keeping records. Let's hope they match ours. We need to see results.

Jesus lived a life of giving. At the end, He gave His life away for us. He was sent from God to us as an evangelism expert. Even in His last hours with the chosen few, He assured them there would be a successor, a comforter, the Holy Spirit who would lead them.

In His day, the sinners, those who were basket cases, those who had made a mess of their lives one way or another, sought after Him. He even ate with them. Now you know that "ruined His testimony," they murmured. Religious people wrote Him off their special lists of friends. But I believe that *Jesus loved hanging out with the down and outers.* He even worked on forming relationships with them.

Some churches don't make a place in their ranks for the outcasts who don't seem to fit in, dress right, or act like us. It takes risks, but it will work. The church should have drunks, drug addicts, prostitutes, crooks, and evil people attending, so that Jesus can be presented to them.

If they won't come to us, let's take the message to the street, the jail, the mission, the prison, and the tavern. We know our purpose; let's have the passion. Maybe we should befriend more of these. That's what evangelism is about.

> *You can't win them if you don't associate with them.*

Maybe you're saying that the Bible tells us to be separate from the world. It means not to act like them, not to isolate yourself. Let's reach out and touch others around us.

You may be thinking that no matter how you stir or rearrange the eggs, if they are rotten, they won't make a good omelet. But how can we win the lost if we don't reach out to them? We must have faith that God can still change lives (Heb. 11:6). Remember how you were before God found you? Most of us are not at all proud of our past.

First, people must like *you* before they will like Jesus and turn their lives over to Him. Let's attract those who need help.

> *God sent Jesus into this world to die for pieces of dirt like us.*

It's been 2,000 years since Jesus came to this planet. He had no back-up plan then and He doesn't have one today. The early church preached everywhere — on the street, in the marketplace. Why? Because they had a passion, and understood what evangelism really is.

I used to think Christians didn't want to win the lost for Christ, but I've come to realize over the years that they really want to win others, but some don't know how to get started. I believe this book will help and guide you if you have a passion to win others to Christ.

The "average" Christian goes through his entire life without leading anyone to Christ. You should be better than average. Forget the status quo. Don't be run-of-the-mill. Everyone is different — but strive for excellence. Let God use you.

Evangelical Christians are, in many respects, well above average. While they only comprise five percent of the population, they have an interesting profile:

29 percent have a college degree (higher than the national average).

68 percent are married; 29 percent have been divorced at least once.

50 percent have children under 18 living in their household.

58 percent are politically conservative.

50 percent live in the south.

45 percent are baby boomers; they are five times less likely than others to say that their "career comes first."

92 percent say that they are "deeply spiritual."

92 percent are concerned about the moral condition of the nation (compared to 74 percent of all adults).

62 percent are concerned about the future.[1]

It will thrill me if you catch the vision of reaching the lost. If you do have a vision and a passion, I hope this book will inspire you, giving you new ideas to do more for God.

Understand the message of evangelism. Hear the voice of Jesus. Your life will be revolutionized.

Endnotes
1 Statistics gathered from <www.barna.org>

CHAPTER 2

YOUR MOTIVES

What is your motivation for winning others to Christ? What do you believe will be the final fate of those who do not accept Christ as their Savior?

There is a general tendency to believe that all "good" people will go to heaven, that people can earn their way into heaven. And only 31 percent believe in a literal, actual hell.

When we believe what Jesus said, "I am the way, the truth and the life, *no man comes to the father but by me,*" it has to make a difference in how we look at the necessity of sharing our faith and bringing others to Christ.

People need to examine their motives. Before a church can explode in growth, leadership has to lead the way.

> *Everyone's life leans in the direction of his/her most dominant thoughts.*

Every waking moment, my mind thinks "winning people to Christ." I can't help it. Wherever I am, it's automatic. It's a passion; it's my purpose for being here.

Pastors know that when I am introduced, I am going to urge others to win people to Christ. They know I'm going to talk about one-on-one soul winning, regardless of the subject I'm speaking on.

Things happen every day of my life, so I continue to have new events to talk about. I pass these ideas on to help others do the same.

Is your motive to really touch lives? Or is it just to be able to brag about how many you've won? Is it to talk about how many are coming to your church?

I love to laugh, to have clean fun, but many times I cry when I see Christians with no passion for the lost. Over the years, I have been to a couple of churches where I have been asked not to give an invitation for the lost. One pastor even stated that it might offend someone. OF COURSE, THESE CHURCHES ARE NEVER ON MY SCHEDULE AGAIN.

Now, I know that people can make a commitment to Christ without ever answering an "altar call." The church grew for many centuries before formal invitations were ever issued from the pulpit, but it seems that in this era, they are a very effective method of bringing about a public stand for Christ. They do not lessen the necessity of nurturing the person as they learn to live their new faith.

We don't always know our real motives, much less the motives of others. One lady with whom I was in a jury pool had this comment, "I can't make decisions about my own life. Why do they want me to decide about someone else?"

We tend to be quick to judge others. We don't always check out the facts. Paul told us that we can feel differently about things and still be members of Christ's Church (Rom. 14:6).

In the past, there have been times I tried to win souls to Christ almost in a competition mode. I wanted to beat last month's record. This was not a good reason for witnessing. My motive should have been simply to win others because they needed God. It is today.

We must not only have a passion and proper motives, we also need a plan and a purpose. We are here for a purpose and need a burning passion to use God's plan to love people. We are at war against the devil on a daily basis. It's life or death.

> *I trust your motives are pure and filled with love, and that you have a real passion to touch the suffering, the hurting and the lost.*

We have a responsibility to share our faith with others. That responsibility should not be a heavy burden, it should be a joy. Because we know what we have been delivered from, and the blessings that He has given us, we should have no problem with the thought that we have a responsibility to be His witnesses.

CHAPTER 3

YOUR PERSONALITY

We are not clones; we don't all do things the same way others do. God didn't make us out of a single mold. We have to work things out — the details, etc., according to who *we* are and who we are trying to win. We may have to step out of our comfort zone.

There are four basic types of personalities. Most of us are a combination of two (or more) of these types. Each type has certain strengths and certain weaknesses. (I have included a chart on page 33.)

When people hear me, some of them say, "I want to be able to do it like Ken." I may give you ideas, but *please* don't try to be me (or Billy Graham, Lowell Lundstrom, Phil Derstine, Dave Williams, or anyone else). Learn to be who *you* are; just be the most effective *you* that you can be.

When people come to me and tell me they wish they had my personality, it really bothers me. I jokingly ask, "If you had *my* personality, would I still have one?" They think they could win lots of people to Christ if they were me. It's a cop-out.

My mind moves in the direction of soul winning. I was even thinking "souls" when I was with a pastor visiting his son in a beautiful Catholic hospital. He was talking to a nurse as we came in. There was a statue of Mary with one hand reaching out as if in blessing and the other hand open. As I passed, I put some tracts into her open hand.

Later, as we left the hospital, I pointed to the statue and said, "Look, Mary is passing out tracts." He laughed and commented that he had never seen that before.

Sunday, he told his congregation they had better get busy witnessing. He said that "in the Catholic hospital, a statue of Mary was passing out tracts." I have never told him that I put them there. When he reads this book, I guess he will find out that I did it.

Check out your personality. You know your strengths and weaknesses. Decide you want to change — desire to change — take the step of faith to change. The power of this personal development is awesome. Be honest with yourself.

Some people have objections to some approaches to winning people. There are others who are turned off (and I can see why) by some approaches. We should all develop the ability to relate and learn how to win others without giving offense.

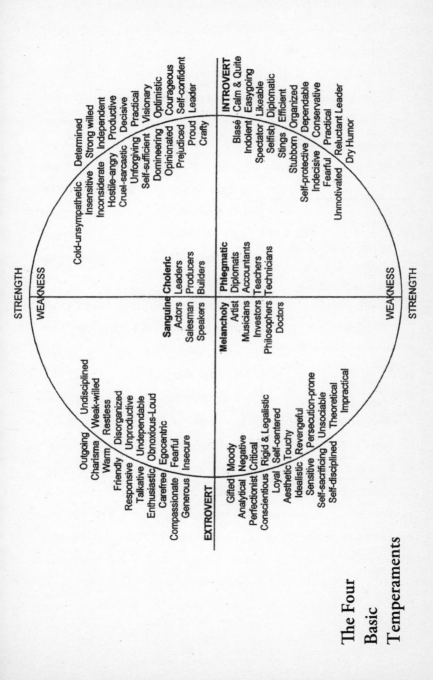

The Four
Basic
Temperaments

Sometimes I tell someone, "You'd make a great soul winner!" The first thing some of them do is give me excuses why they can't.

There are times that I use the question "Are you a Christian?" as a witnessing tool with a waitress or waiter. If they say, "Yes," I might ask him or her how many they win to Christ each month.

If they say "No, and why do you ask?" I state, "You have a nice smile and great personality. You could help many hurting people." I've led several wait staff to Christ with this approach (see Chapter 17).

In Phil Derstine's book, *Evangelism That Works*, he talks about relationship evangelism. He also advocates getting out of the church and onto the street as the most effective method of evangelism.

I realize that it's more than a smile and a good personality that count, but that does open the door to witnessing.

Don't try to be a professional. It's okay to be an amateur. Remember, amateurs built Noah's ark — professionals built the Titanic.

For more personality or temperament study, I highly recommend the writings of Tim or Beverly LaHaye, or Florence Litauer.

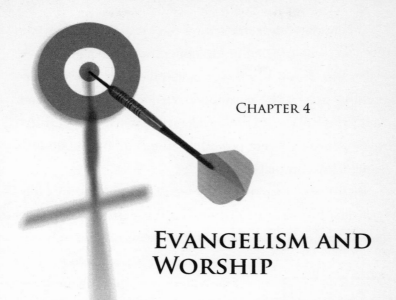

EVANGELISM AND WORSHIP

Worship and witnessing are Siamese twins. Where you have one, you have the other. If the worship doesn't turn you into a dynamo witness machine, something is very wrong. Vice versa.

The term "worship" means many things to many people. No single interpretation of the word is common to more than one out of five adults in this country. The most likely definitions relate to expressions of praise or thanks, praying, attending church services, an attitude toward God, a personal relationship with God, or holy living. If you worship, you won't worry and stew and fret.

> *Yea, though I walk through the valley of the shadow of death, I will fear no evil: for thou art with me; thy rod and thy staff they comfort me.*
>
> Psalm 23:4

When the Holy Spirit fell on the Day of Pentecost, the 120 who were gathered in the upper room had a great time of worship. It was so good that it spilled out into the surrounding streets. The worship attracted lots of attention, and Peter (who had denied his Lord less than two months earlier) began to preach a very powerful sermon. About 3,000 embraced Christ on that day (Acts 2:40–47).

By the way, there is a really logical reason that the Holy Spirit first baptized the disciples on this particular day. The Jewish Feast of Weeks, which we call Pentecost, not only celebrated the harvest, it celebrated the giving of the Mosaic law. Think about it, the Law provided the power for Judaism.

> The Holy Spirit is the only source of power for Christians.

I believe writing my checks to my home church for tithes, offerings, missions, or whatever, is a form of worship. It's not just to help the church bring in more money than the previous year. I feel the presence of God when I write these checks. I also feel thankfulness that He has supplied the funds for my needs; the least I can do is give Him His portion.

When we worship during the "worship" portion of the service, it should do more than just make us feel good. It should stir up a passion for the lost. I know it "turns me on," and "lights my fire."

On the other hand, when I witness to people about knowing Christ (not getting religion,) it's a form of worship.

So I believe that *evangelism and worship go hand in hand*. Rick Warren, pastor of Saddleback Church in Southern California, states that our worship should attract sinners. It should not be a time in the service that just makes us feel good, it should be a time when the presence of God can be felt by the entire congregation — both those who are committed to Christ, and those who aren't.

The item rated most important by the most Christians is the ability to worship. Some of the terms used to describe their church's worship were inspiring, refreshing, Spirit-filled, challenging, and life transforming.

The anointing should strengthen us for service and witnessing for the coming week. I know that after a morning service, I leave so charged up that I can hardly wait to witness.

Dave Williams of Lansing, Michigan, says that when people's hearts are "plowed up" by worship, they will be more receptive to win souls.

Phil Derstine's youth group at Christian Retreat in Bradenton, Florida, started a "Hell House" at Halloween with a very scary exhibit. Thousands of teenagers waited hours in line to hear the gospel presented with shocking reality.

Phil called it "unconventional soul winning." Even the major networks — ABC, NBC, CBS, and CNN — covered it. This didn't sound like evangelism and worship, but it goes hand in hand.

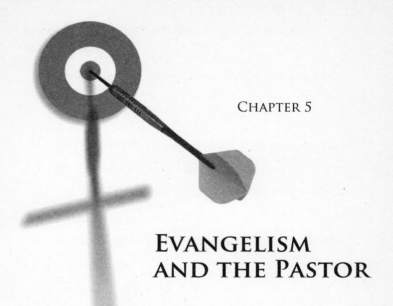

CHAPTER 5

EVANGELISM AND THE PASTOR

Often the big "crash programs" don't cut it. They end up looking good for the church, but don't produce much of a harvest. We should take a long look at our failing programs, our carnal ways, our ego trips and ask God for a genuine revival. Our interest should be in a revolutionized society, not just in church growth.

George Barna has been researching churches since 1984. His website is used as a source reference throughout this

> *We get so busy with programs that we're bogged down in a wilderness of ineffectiveness. We talk about a God of dynamite while we live little firecracker lives. The devil laughs at our frustration.*

book (www.barna.org). He revealed the following in a recent interview.

There are five significant changes or trends in the church:

1. There is a decline in biblical literacy. Fewer and fewer people have any clue what the Bible really teaches as opposed to what they feel it should teach.

2. There is an increased emphasis on mega-churches. There is stress on numbers rather than the transformation of lives.

3. There is a rise of the importance of para-church ministry. Much of what churches used to do has been taken over by para-church ministries.

4. There is an increased negativity of the media toward Christianity.

5. Church members seem to rely upon the paid clergy to do the ministry, instead of the laity working to get things done.

If trends continue, within the next 20 years, there will be:

1. A decreased involvement in church-based ministry.

2. An increased diversity of forms of churches — more house-churches (like cell groups) — more places of worship that are not "church."

3. More denominations because of splits.

4. Different expectations in denominational ministry. Changes will occur because of the new generation of leadership — different orientation to relationship and institutions — if they don't meet expectations, they will not exist.

In Dave Williams's book, *Supernatural Soulwinning*, he discusses how history reveals that within the first 200 years of Christianity, the entire known world heard the gospel.[1] Paul tells us that this actually happened in less than 30 years.

The gospel of Jesus Christ was bringing forth fruit in all the known world by A.D. 62. The first church after Jesus died, was buried, and ascended into heaven, reached the entire world in one generation. Yes, down through the centuries, entire cities were reached.

Remember these names: John Wesley, George Whitfield, Jonathan Edwards, Charles Finney, D.L. Moody, Smith Wigglesworth, Billy Sunday, Billy Graham?

God moved in real revival. Taverns closed. Police departments closed so that officers could attend prayer and revival meetings.

Jesus wanted His followers to be able to hear Him as He talked to God (Luke 11:1–11; Matt. 6:9–13).

We know that knowledge alone is not enough. We have to have action. Great "disciplers" are very intentional, aggressive, and passion-driven about what they want to accomplish, feeding their vision to their workers.

When it is all boiled down, those of us who are seeking to train people must be prepared and know how to teach them to follow us, even as we follow Christ (1 Cor. 11:1).

Some churches are so busy having church that they never attempt to win souls. Paul said:

> *"Join with others in following my example, brothers, and take note of those who live according to the pattern we gave you."*
>
> *Phil. 3:17; NIV*

We are the exhibit, and given time, it is possible to impart our way of living to those who are constantly with us. Many pastors and other friends cultivate a relationship with me in order to learn from me (not that I know everything, by a long shot). We always talk about what God is doing in different places. We talk often just to report a meeting, or we exchange ideas.

Relationships are not just one way.

Jesus told His team to go and that He would enable them to get the job done (Matt. 10:1; Mark 6:7; Mark 16:15; Luke 9:1–2). If they were not well received, He told them to shake off the dust as a witness against those who did not receive them (Matt 10:14–15; Mark 6:11; Luke 9:5). Jesus never let His followers underestimate the enemy's power. He told them to be wise, because He was sending them as sheep among wolves (Matt. 10:16).

In some areas around the world, churches are growing so fast that they can hardly keep up with the growth. Sunday morning, evening, and many nights during the week, the crowds are coming to hear the gospel. These are "on fire" churches.

Other churches close by are only a place for Christians to meet and fellowship with one another, not a place of evangelism. It's no wonder that some of the world is ignoring the places where nothing is happening. Some churches seem to be trying to regroup to find their own destiny.

In churches where people are praying and seeking God "big time," something is happening. I don't mean just a couple of dozen folks in the prayer room. When I see a church where the lobby is buzzing with people visiting, drinking coffee, and talking about everything but Jesus before the worship services, I check out the prayer room.

Sometimes not one person is there. In many of the churches where I minister, hundreds are coming an hour early to pray before the services. A good example of this is Countryside Christian Center in Clearwater, Florida, where John Lloyd is pastor.

It simply boils down to a passion for the lost. No wonder these churches are exploding for God. They evidently understand 2 Chronicles 7:14: "If my people 1) pray, 2) and seek my face, 3) and turn from their wicked ways," God will forgive and heal us.

The church has its programs, organizational skills, crusades, special events, and sometimes nothing happens. I'm not talking against their efforts, because the church would not exist without them. Winning the world is not usually done by some new program, but by people who reach out and touch people.

> *It was God's plan for us to have power.*

We are the church (Matt. 16:18). God again is calling pastors and people (who can hear His call) with a passion, a vision, a dream, a plan, a goal, and, of course, purpose. Men and women are God's method of winning the world. The world is looking for leaders to follow. They will follow someone who is actually leading.

Jesus had followers because he was able to deliver. He was a real leader.

Everyone should have a chance, under their pastor, for some type of evangelism training, perhaps using James Kennedy's book *Evangelism Explosion,* or a similar course. Training and leadership should come through the pastor. We must move from just "church vision," to "kingdom vision." (Some pastors have told me they plan to use this book.)

We don't need a slick, high-powered salesperson to win people. We need regular folks who have been taught how and will bathe their efforts in prayer. You can spend years trying to win someone, but it takes prayer to make it succeed. After a ten-day prayer meeting, Peter led 3,000 to Christ with one sermon.

> *The difference between a protégé and a parasite is that a protégé wants what's in your mind and in your heart, a parasite wants what's in your hand.*

We need the power, the vision, the knowledge, the plan, and above all the passion to win a world to Christ. The disciples had the greatest teacher. I'm sure they were impressed. He turned everything into a lesson for them. Jesus' method during His first year was to teach the disciples. He led them into a relationship with God. He knew they would need that relationship with the Father. The day would come when He would be bodily gone and they would be "in charge." Now they needed supervision.

Today, it's the same. People need supervision in *how to evangelize*. The plan is the same now as in Jesus' day. It's not the number we win, but the ones we disciple to win others. Remember, there is no back-up plan. God wants us to reproduce. If we are not really trained to win through our leaders:

> *We can only reproduce what we are.*

Some churches don't grow because they don't evangelize and are not taught how to use a plan that works. Others use outdated, ineffective methods. We should teach by example (1 Cor. 4:16).

We think that we are really "hot stuff," really tight with God. But according to George Barna, "We are the church of Laodicea, and we haven't a clue what is going on." He says that "the biggest deception is that we really don't care."

Some believe evangelism is to herd as many as you can in to hear the pastor, and hope he catches a few of them. Isn't the pastor the big fisherman?

I don't believe that the primary job of the senior pastor is to be the major soul winner. The pastor is the shepherd. Sheep bear sheep. But some think the pastor can ambush some new sheep, maybe even mug (or trick) them some way.

Others try to pull new fish out of other churches. They aren't really fishing, they are trying to steal fish from other bowls to put into their own fishbowl.

Some believe that evangelism is what Billy and Franklin Graham do, and they should do it all by themselves. They think they can't compete with them, so why try at all?

> The pastor's role is very important

What kind of people do we want in the church? In my seminar, *The Main Thing Is to Keep the Main Thing the Main Thing,* usually held on Saturday, I teach: What kind of pastors produce these kinds of people? What kind of team can do this? What kind of pastor makes this team possible?

We actually become like those we spend the most time with. A pastor has to teach people. He must create a climate for real growth. He has to love people the way they are, and the people must love the pastors (warts and all), and the people need to love one another. Together, we all share our faith, winning our area to Christ and touching the world.

No church will grow and prosper if the pastors, board, deacons, elders, and all the others with a position of authority, are not all working together in love. Love and unity and not seeking our own interest are important (1 Cor. 13:4–7). We have to talk, walk, act, love, and care like dedicated leaders (1 Tim. 3:1–16; 1 Pet. 5:2). It has to come from a heart of passion.

Being accountable is also very important. Accountability is missing in some churches today. The joys of relationships are very exciting, so we need relationships and accountability. Church gossiping, jockeying for position, family quarrels, manipulation, and politics never work.

I believe that Christians can sponsor non-religious community events to love and touch the lives of the unbeliever. One of my good friends, Jeff Knight, pastors the Rock Church in Monroe, Washington. That church owns a race car that races regionally. It's a chance to get out among unbelievers as a witness. How exciting!

> *Love and unity always work.*

At Stone Church, where I attend when I'm home, Pastor Jon Oletzke has a special day for classic cars and motorcycles. It's another outreach to our community. You may or may not like this. Let me ask you, "How many did you lead to Christ this week?"

> *God is highly concerned about the*
> *quality a leader shows.*

If we are to win this world to Christ, we need an army who loves. Also, one which is above reproach in every way (Acts 6:3; 1 Tim. 3:2; Titus 1:6–7).

I'm not taking snipes at others, but in all honesty, I must say it upsets me when some so-called leaders who have had several wives, are trying to teach others how to live. I saw a preacher on Christian TV just the other day talk about the miracles in his life that happen when he prays. He's on his third wife since he entered the ministry. I have a hard time respecting either him or his ministry and sometimes even those who are his close associates (1 Tim 3:2, 7). How can he tell others to obey God, when his own life is a mess?

I know God forgives, but I think people need to be able to say that they see something very different and wonderful about you, your life, your family, and that your marriage is so good. That's why you should want to be like Christ.

> *Your*
> *testimony*
> *should be*
> *so good,*
> *they want*
> *to be like*
> *you.*

The Jews had a rule for each day. We can draw up our own set of do's and don'ts. Some spend all their time preaching against overeating, movies, smoking, alcohol, and even coffee or Coca-cola.

Maybe drinking coffee is wrong for you, because you don't do it in moderation. It may not be wrong for me, since I usually have a cup of coffee or two a day. I don't have to have caffeine to be able to function, like some who are hooked on it. It can become as addictive as drugs or alcohol; then it's wrong. If we can't begin to function in the morning without our caffeine, we're probably addicted. We need to be careful how we judge.

Some come from a negative past where they were programmed to fail. There are many excuses, but we need to look for ways with relationships, prayer, and simply reaching out in friendship to touch our world. We can either judge or love others. We can't do both. We need love. Love speaks truth.

We should be open and transparent. No one is perfect, no church is perfect, no pastor is perfect. We only know of one perfect man, and His name is Jesus.

A real leader should be able to lead others to answers in their lives. Our ministry has a wonderful board of directors. We don't always agree on everything. If we all agreed all the time, there would be no need for a board. We have to discuss things and work together in love, and we do. Sometimes all but one will agree, but that person makes us think — maybe we should look at something in a different way.

You've heard about the want ad for a new minister, I'm sure:

WANTED

Minister for growing church. A real opportunity for the right man. Opportunity to become better acquainted with people.

Applicant must offer experience as shop worker, office manager, educator (all levels, including college), artist, salesman, diplomat, writer, theologian, politician, Boy Scout leader, children's worker, minor league athlete, psychologist, vocational counselor, psychiatrist, funeral director, wedding consultant, master of ceremonies, circus clown, missionary, social worker. Helpful but not essential: experience as a butcher, baker, cowboy, Western Union messenger.

Must know all about problems of birth, marriage, and death; also conversant with the latest theories and practices in areas like pediatrics, economics, and nuclear science.

Right man will hold firm views on every topic, but is careful not to upset people who disagree. Must be forthright but flexible: returns criticism and backbiting with Christian love and forgiveness. Should have outgoing, friendly disposition at all times. Should be captivating speaker and intent listener. Will pretend he enjoys hearing women talk.

Education must be beyond Ph.D requirements, but always concealed in homespun modesty and folksy talk. Able to sound learned at times but most of the time talks and acts like good-old-Joe. Familiar with literature read by average congregation.

Must be willing to work long hours, subject to call anytime of day or night, adaptable to sudden interruption. Will spend at least 25 hours preparing sermons. Additional 10 hours reading books and magazines.

Applicant's wife must be both stunning and plain, smartly attired but conservative in appearance, gracious and able to get along with everyone, especially women. Must be willing to work in church kitchen, teach Sunday school, operate computer, wait tables, never listen to gossip, never become discouraged.

Applicant's children must be exemplary in conduct and character; well-behaved, yet basically no different from other children, decently dressed.

Opportunity for applicant to live close to work. Furnished home provided, open door hospitality enforced. Must be ever mindful the house does not belong to him.

Directly responsible for views and conduct to all church members and visitors, not confined to direction or support from any one person. Salary not commensurate with experience or need; no overtime pay. All replies kept confidential. Anyone applying will undergo full investigation to determine sanity.

My pastor, Jon Oletzke, is a great and effective pastor, and my friend. Like the rest of us, he is not perfect, he is not God, but he is my pastor. He does the job of ministry that God has called him to do. He doesn't try to copy others. He has passion for the lost, a genuine love for people, and is able to talk to total strangers. He lets people know that God is alive and well and willing to help us. He is probably one of the most transparent men I know.

Pastors that I associate with are the best. However, in many cases, working with uncommitted people must be discouraging. They must be concerned at times of what people think and say. Some are lonely. They also need a close friend that they can talk to.

Most books on being a pastor should be hauled to the dump. Every Sunday, give your pastor and his wife a hug and tell them how much you appreciate them. It might also be good to do that to all the staff members and maybe even the ushers.

> *Some churches are sinking ships.*

First, nothing is happening and that's why no one shows up Sunday night. So then they cancel Sunday night service. Christians seem happy, but the world doesn't see anything happening. In some churches where I minister, their Sunday nights are like their Sunday mornings, full of people worshiping God. There are always exceptions.

In other areas, churches have Saturday night and multiple Sunday mornings but no Sunday night, and the church is growing by leaps and bounds.

In some areas around the world, churches are growing so fast that they can hardly keep up with the growth. Sunday morning, evening, and many nights during the week, the crowds are coming to hear the gospel.

They will go where they feel they can find it. Cell (or small) groups on Sunday nights are working some places, and the church is growing. In other areas, the church is not growing, it is declining in spite of its cell groups, which sometimes cause them to lose the vision of what they really

> *People are crying out for love and looking for answers.*

are all about. The church seems to be an institution that is slow to learn. We don't see the ship sinking until it's too late.

A church was burning down, fire trucks were trying to put out the blaze. A man who lived across the street came over to watch. He was a professed atheist and had never been on this church property (also never invited), and was laughing about the church burning. The pastor said to him, "I've never seen you over here before." He replied, *"Your church has never been on fire before."*

There you have it.

Some churches have special classes for adults on government affairs, how to get a job, cooking classes, how to know where the best sales are, even craft classes on costume jewelry, but they have never offered any *classes on how to win others to Jesus.* They don't have a "kingdom vision." There are some leaders in each church who could teach it.

In one church where I minister every year, they have a 12-week soul winning course. The first 6 weeks are classroom teaching; the final 6 weeks are on the streets, led by the pastor.

We teach that everyone in church should know the essentials, but we have never taught them what they really are. Children (and adults) should be taught what the essential doctrines of the church are. Many times they say only what they think we want them to say.

A Sunday school class of second graders was asked what gathers nuts in the fall, is fuzzy, has a bushy tail, and climbs trees. One little boy said, "It sounds like a squirrel to me, but I know you want me to say it's Jesus."

There are definitely some generational differences within the church. We'll use the standard classifications of *Seniors* (born before 1927), *Builders* (1927–1945), *Boomers* (1946–1964), and *Busters* (1965–1983).

Busters appear to be the least evangelized, volunteer less, participate less, attend church less, report praying less, place less importance upon their faith, and believe in an all-powerful God. They seem to be searching more for the meaning of life, feel that they are too overwhelmed.

By contrast, the percentages of the other three groups is significantly greater in each of the areas mentioned above. Perhaps many of these differences occur because of a lack of maturity in the Busters, and we need to focus more effort on our young adults. It would seem that the church dropped the ball somewhere along the line.

People are not really trained to think. Everyone knows that in my meetings I work on helping people to think. I have asked the silly question, "If you had a truck with ten calves and nine goats, how old would the driver be?" Eighty percent answered 19. They certainly are not thinking.

We've heard the story of the "Frog in the Kettle." George Barna even wrote a book with that title.[2] He contends that the church is just like that frog.

The frog sat in the bowl of room temperature water; the heat is turned up a little at a time. The frog stays in the kettle, unaware of what is actually happening, just as happy as if it had good sense. Finally, the water comes to a boil and the frog dies. The moral of this is that the frog is content to the end, which in this case is death. We might learn from the frog.

Endnotes
1 Dave Williams, *Supernatural Soulwinning*.
2 George Barna, *Frog in the Kettle* (Ventura, CA: Regal Books, 1990).

Chapter 6

Fishing

Don't tell people what they need to change in order to become a Christian. When a person accepts Christ, he becomes a new creature. God will clean him up; he will change for the better (believe it or not, without your help).

Don't tell him how to dress, what friends to get rid of, or what music is accept-able. Bad habits will fall off. Truth will set them free. The Hebrew word for *truth* is *emet* — the root verb which means to be firm, secure, and solid.

> *Some of us Christians try to clean our fish before we catch them.*

Here's a modern parable:

Now it came to pass that a group existed who called themselves *Fishermen*. And lo, there were many fish in the waters all around. In fact, the whole area was surrounded by streams and lakes filled with fish. And the fish were hungry.

Week after week, month after month, and year after year, those who called themselves Fishermen met in meetings and talked about their call to fish, the abundance of fish, and how they might go about fishing.

Year after year, they carefully defined what fishing means, defended fishing as an occupation, and declared that fishing is always to be a primary task of Fishermen. Continually they searched for new and better methods of fishing. Further they said, "The fishing industry exists by fishing as fire exists by burning."

They sponsored meetings called *Fishermen's Campaigns* and *The Month for Fishermen to Fish*. They sponsored costly nationwide and worldwide congresses to discuss fishing and to promote fishing and hear all the ways of fishing, such as new fishing equipment, fish calls, and whether a new bait was discovered.

These Fishermen built large, beautiful buildings called Fishermen's Headquarters. The plea was that everyone should be a Fisherman and every Fisherman should fish. One thing they didn't do, however; *they didn't fish*.

In addition to meeting regularly, they organized a board of directors to send out Fishermen to other places where there were many fish. All the Fishermen seemed to agree that what was needed was a board that could challenge Fishermen to be faithful in fishing. The board was formed of those who had great vision and courage to speak about fishing, to define fishing, and to promote the idea of fishing in faraway streams and lakes where many other fish of different colors lived.

Also, the board hired staff members and appointed other boards and held many meetings to defend fishing and to decide what new streams should be considered.

But the staff and board members still did not fish.

Large, elaborate, and expensive training centers were built whose original and primary purpose was to teach Fishermen how to fish. Over the years, courses were offered on the needs of fish, the nature of fish, where to find fish, the psychological reactions of fish, and how to approach and feed fish.

Those who taught had the doctorates in fishology. *But the teachers did not fish.* They only taught fishing. Year after year, after tedious training, many were graduated and given fishing licenses.

Some spent much study and travel to learn the history of fishing and to see faraway places where the founding fathers did great fishing in the centuries past. They lauded the faithful Fishermen of years before who handed down the idea of fishing.

Further, the Fishermen built large printing houses to publish fishing guides. Presses were kept busy day and night to produce materials solely devoted to fishing methods, equipment, and programs to arrange and to encourage meetings to talk about fishing. A speakers' bureau was also provided to schedule special speakers on the subject of fishing.

Many who felt the call to be Fishermen responded. They were commissioned and sent to fish. But like the Fishermen back home, they never *fished*.

Like the Fishermen back home, they engaged in all kinds of other occupations. They built power plants to pump water for fish and tractors to plow new waterways. They made all kinds of equipment to travel here and there to look at fish hatcheries.

Some also said they wanted to be part of the fishing party, and they felt called to furnish fishing equipment. Others felt their job was to relate to the fish in a good way, so the fish would know the difference between good and bad Fishermen. Others felt that simply letting the fish know they were nice, land-loving neighbors was enough.

After one stirring meeting on "The Necessity of Fishing," a young fellow left the meeting and *went fishing*. The next day, he reported that he had caught two outstanding fish. He was honored for his excellent catch and scheduled to visit all the big meetings possible to tell how he did it. So, *he quit his fishing* in order to have time to tell about the experience to other fishermen. He was also placed on the Fishermen's general board as a person having considerable experience.

Now it's true that many of the Fishermen sacrificed and put up with all kinds of difficulties. Some lived near the water and bore the smell of dead fish every day. They received the ridicule of some who made fun of the Fishermen's clubs and the fact that they claimed to be Fishermen, *yet never fished*.

They wondered about those who felt it was of little use to attend the weekly meetings to talk about fishing. After all, were they not following the Master who said, "Follow me, and I will make you fishers of men?"

Imagine how hurt some were when one day a person suggested that those who didn't catch fish were really not Fishermen, no matter how much they claimed to be. Yet it did sound correct. Is a person a Fisherman if year after year he never catches a fish? *Is one following if he isn't fishing?*

My father taught me the following three things about fishing.

First . . . Go where the fish are. If you plan to catch fish, go where the fish are. Don't get up at four o'clock in the morning on a cold day, get all dressed, and go stand on a riverbank unless you want to catch fish. If you don't plan to catch fish, stay home and drop your line in the bathtub.

Second . . . Don't scare them before you catch them. As a boy, I used to throw rocks in the water. Dad would scold me and tell me I was scaring all the fish away. So if the plan is to actually catch fish, we can't scare them. After the fish are in the net, you can laugh at them, make faces at them, smile at them, sing to them, or try to teach them Hebrew. (What I'm saying is, don't scare the fish.) With fish, it doesn't matter after you catch them. With people, you still need to nurture them and let the Holy Spirit do the clean up job.

Third . . . If your bait isn't working, change it. Some church folks say, "This is the way we have always done it before. We always sang out of the hymnbook, we didn't sing choruses or use PowerPoint. We always used cloth bags instead of offering plates or buckets. We always used the King James Bible, not one of those new versions. The last pastor didn't do it that way! Why change now?"

But if what you're doing isn't working, if you're not making an impact in your area, maybe you should "change the bait."

You can change your methods without changing your principles. That's what Jesus teaches in the fifth chapter of Luke. Jesus also had a plan.

Jesus was at the Sea of Galilee, and He had just finished speaking to the people when He turned to Simon Peter and said 13 famous words, "Launch out into the deep and let down your nets for a draught."

Jesus knew that Simon had failed. He knew he had fished all night without catching any fish. Jesus didn't discuss it, or even mention it. It was a past failure that was worthless to worry about. This is a lesson for all of us. Jesus didn't even ask Simon if he wanted to go fishing.

Simon was also aware he had failed the night before, and he began to make excuses, as many do. He talked about the failure. Even with Jesus in the boat, I'm not really sure Simon expected to catch anything. He said, "We'll let down the nets," not, "We'll catch fish."

The Sea of Galilee is approximately 6 miles wide, 13 miles long, and 150 feet deep at its deepest. They usually fished in the shallower north end where the Jordan flows in and there are warm springs and the fish feed there. They always fished at night.

Let's consider the approach that Jesus took. It was a completely new concept.

Jesus told him <u>what to do</u> — to go fishing in the daytime.

He told him <u>how to do it</u> — to let down his nets on the other side of the boat.

He told him <u>where to do it</u> — out in the deep where he would not expect to find fish.

He also told him he would be a success, when he had previously failed.

He had the whole plan laid out for Simon Peter. Because Peter decided to follow the plan, he found *those who attempt the unusual often achieve the impossible if they listen to the Master.*

If I drive from Yakima to Seattle, the road is already laid out. But it is shorter "as the crow flies." So why don't I take off over the river and through the woods? I could say, "I don't care what others have done, I know a short cut. I'll do it my way." If I try it my way, I just plain won't get there.

Jesus was saying to Simon, "Your plan was a total flop. Now follow My plan and be a success. Scrap your plan and do it My way."

If your program and plan isn't working, maybe you need to listen. You have heard the saying, "Don't change horses in the middle of the stream." But if your horse is dead, you better get off and get another horse.

God's plans work. He knows where the fish are today. Follow His plan, and you'll succeed. God has the answers.

> *To be a fisherman, you have to catch fish. It doesn't matter if you have a boat, how much tackle and equipment you have, or if you live by the lake. You must catch fish to be considered a fisherman.*

One . . . if it isn't working, scrap your old program.

Two . . . do it His way.

Three . . . don't ask God to bless what you are doing; instead, do what He's blessing.

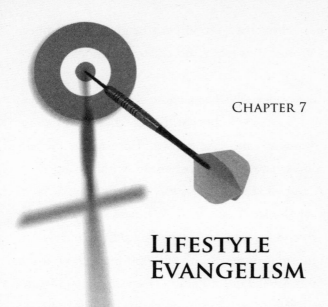

CHAPTER 7

LIFESTYLE EVANGELISM

It's wonderful to preach to the masses. However, preparing and training leaders for the winning of souls all over the world has been a thrill for me. Training 1,400 leaders in India will never be forgotten. We talk a lot about evangelism, but it does involve follow-up and personal attention. This takes a lot of time. A haphazard follow-up will not work.

Jesus trained 12 men and gave them His personal attention. These were the men who would carry on after His death. Jesus paired up the disciples (both the 12 and the 70) two by two, so they could have fellowship and help from each other. He gave them power over the devil (Luke 10:1, 17).

Some authors have tried to paint a picture in our minds of these disciples. We wonder why Jesus concentrated on just the Twelve. A leader just teaches you how to follow. He knew that more effective attention can be given to members of a smaller group. People do and teach the things they see and hear.

I used to wonder why Jesus chose to only touch a few when He came here to win the world. Why didn't He choose an army of thousands and take the world overnight? He had all power to do whatever He chose to do, with the angels at His disposal. But all He chose was this unlikely crew of men.

Remember the story of Gideon? (Judges 6–8). God directed him to trim his massive army of 32,000 men down to a mere 300 in order to defeat the 120,000-man army of the Midianites and Amelekites. Often, a few well-trained workers can accomplish more than a multitude of folks who do nothing but get in each other's (and God's) way.

Jesus taught His disciples how to win the world. He showed them with examples. He taught them seed faith (Matt. 17:20). Trees are known by the fruit they bear. He didn't teach them to just attend church, but to be real disciples. They certainly would need to be real disciples if they were to endure until the end (Matt. 24:13).

These men would learn what evangelism was. It would cost them their lives. Some would be boiled in oil; Andrew, Simon, and Peter would be crucified; James would be beheaded. All but one would die violently. Only John would live to a ripe old age.

When Jesus talked sacrifice and death, many walked away from Him. *They left the team* (John 6:25–59, 66). Jesus didn't chase after them to keep them in the fold. When they offered excuses, like needing to conduct a family funeral, He told them to "let the dead bury the dead" (Matt 8:21–22).

He also admonished them to "go and preach the kingdom of God" (Luke 9:60). Many want to do their own thing, but know nothing of sacrifice. Jesus talked about His death and suffering about 16 times before His arrest. This was not a very pretty thought for His followers.

What is sacrifice? Believers by the thousands marched into Alexandria, Egypt, of their own accord to touch lives during the plague. Some even sold themselves into slavery so they could touch and help other believer slaves.

Thousands of Christians were taken to Rome to be executed as the persecution grew tougher and tougher. *They made the journey into a victory celebration, not a death march*. Now this is sacrifice!

> *Salt preserves, but it is absolutely useless unless it gets out of the container that it's in.*

Sometimes new Christians are taught that they no longer have anything in common with unbelievers. We have a lot in common — unbelievers are people with challenges, payments, a house to keep up, a yard to groom, weight issues, kids to raise, and so on, just like believers.

Some believe that Christians should never have a non-Christian friend, but Jesus set a different example for us: He was a "friend to sinners." That was the worst "insult" the

Pharisees had for Him. It would be good to follow His example.

Our former pastor, Dale Carpenter, realized one day that all of his friends were Christians. He told the congregation that he needed that week to find some pre-Christian friends. He joined a local service club, and in a few words, won several of them to Christ.

God has rescued us from the garbage dump, where Satan left us to die. Now as a royal heir with Christ we have been made whole by the ultimate recycler. We are now part of the nature of God, a piece of clay in the Master's hand. And maybe, if we are teachable, He will make something worthwhile out of us.

You have heard it said that people "Don't care how much you know until they know how much you care."

Not many non-believers are reading the Bible. We are the only Bible they read. Our lives can make the difference between someone spending eternity in heaven or in hell.

I love the *Personal Promise* edition of the Bible that we send to non-believers because their name is inserted in it over 5,000 times.[1] It's a great witnessing tool. People will read it just to find their name. I've even had some pre-Christians order them. I have one myself and have given all my grandkids one.

Jesus was aware of gender barriers. He was kind and open, but didn't choose a woman to be a disciple. It would have been unthinkable in that day. Women were considered second-class citizens, just one step above a slave. The Gospels do make it clear that a number of women did often travel with the disciples, probably cooking and caring for their other practical needs. Jesus defended Mary of Bethany when she chose to listen to Jesus instead of helping her sister, Martha (Luke 10:38–42).

A person who is successful doesn't fight the system unless the system is very wrong. In some areas of the world, religious viewpoint is cultural, not scriptural. In some countries, a woman with pierced ears is not allowed to take communion. The Bible doesn't teach that. That person is now a Christian, a believer, a part of His church, yet she can't take communion. Some of our greatest barriers are cultural, not theological.

Years ago, when we traveled with our musical group, many places the girls could not wear shorts on the church property, but it was okay for the guys to do so.

Some believe that communion should only be served in a church, never in a hospital or at a sickbed. Some believe wives should never work outside the home. Some believe a pastor should always stand behind his pulpit, and never move around. Some believe that no Christian woman should ever wear make-up or jewelry, but must wear a hat in church.

This list could go on and on. Just remember that legalism is wrong. We're talking about relating to our world with lifestyle evangelism.[2] The further you are from personal evangelism, the more likely you will be to criticize others (and maybe even this book).

If you object to Christians befriending non-Christians, you have probably never befriended one yourself.

Here's a scenario — He drinks beer, his wife runs around, the son is in jail, and the daughter is pregnant. Some are taught to avoid people like this. They need love. This family really needs Christian friends. We can't win them if we avoid them.

You may have a good message, a passion to win the lost. Your friends are all Christians; you go to work, then home and back to work, where many times you work with Christians, and eat with them, then you go to church. You seem to make it through every day and have no audience for winning people to Christ, because you haven't built relationships with anyone who needs Christ.

Don't become so different (weird) that no one can relate to you except other Christians. Love is spelled N-E-I-G-H-B-O-R or S-T-R-A-N-G-E-R (Luke 10:25–29). To be different is not to be a snob, or legalistic, but to be like Christ.

Sometimes I've had to say to someone, "I like the way I win souls a lot better than the way you don't."

Sometimes I will take a piece of paper and write down these words: wealth, success, sports cars, happy marriage, fame, children, after death. I ask someone to number these in the order of importance to them. It opens a door for witnessing.

John the Baptist appeared on the scene as a religious nut. He didn't eat bread or drink wine — he only ate locust (carob pods) and wild honey — people said he had a devil. Jesus came befriending sinners and going to parties, and they criticized Him, calling Him a glutton and a drinker (Luke 7:33–35).

People always have to find something to criticize. John and Jesus were radically different, yet both were criticized.

You're either on the building crew or the wrecking crew. On the building crew, you give, help, love, sacrifice, work, lift up, and go out of your way to help others. You become a positive force. On the wrecking crew, you criticize, tear down, spread rumors, and become a negative force.

Paul said that he "became all things to all men" (1 Cor. 9:22). He adjusted his social life when it was appropriate. He didn't use Mosaic law when he was trying to reach Gentiles. He didn't insult their beliefs; he used them as a point of reference.

There are times when we must make some compromise with customs in order not to offend those we are trying to reach. If I am in a very conservative area where it is customary for a speaker to always wear a suit and tie, I probably will do so, even though I normally dress more casually in a sport jacket and sweater. It doesn't upset my theology to conform in this kind of situation.

Sometimes believers view pre-Christians as the enemy. It's no wonder they are uncomfortable with us. A Christian's comfort zone is his Christian sub-culture. We need to get out of our comfort zone to reach the lost. I'm not advocating wild parties and alcohol to "fit in."

Being radically different doesn't mean becoming withdrawn or arrogant. Paul's genuine efforts and methods were made within the framework of local culture.

Many times, I have shown an interest in someone's world, asking questions on an airplane. I know when I'm on a five-hour flight, I should take two or three hours to get to know my seat partner. He and I are "stuck" with each other for a while. The person then becomes receptive to my world, and many times accepts Christ. We need to make ourselves flexible to other people's cultures and situations, without compromising our moral principles.

> *A slave always meets the need of others.*

Paul made his body a slave to win others. He does whatever needs to be done. If a car needs cleaning, he becomes a detail man. If someone is sick, he becomes a nurse. If someone is a fisherman, he talks fishing. You get my drift.

The lifestyle of the main leadership in a church usually flows down to others. I could name many of my close pastor friends here. Many of them call me weekly to exchange ideas on winning souls.

We have to be relevant in this hour. A third grader was asked what they did in Sunday school. He replied that the teacher talks and the kids just sit. George Barna, the church researcher stated that most Sunday schools do not provide the quality of teaching and experience that people demand these days in exchange for their time.

If we want to win the world, maybe we'd better start at home. It seems in this generation that some parents don't really care about their kids. TV, computers, and inappropriate music are what are important to kids today. Dad and Mom are busy making money. They leave the kids unsupervised or with friends. No rules are laid out, or they are laid out but not enforced.

Does your family have daily devotions? People are busy and their real priorities are messed up. Have we forgotten what the real goals are and lost our way? Unless you're a radical soul winner, you won't like this at all. Sometimes we are so concerned about learning the Bible that we forget to make friends or to even be a friend. Many have lost their way.

Sometimes when I am with a pastor who is a great witness, we almost "fight" over who is going to witness to the next person. Years ago, Quentin Edwards and I flew together to Seoul, Korea, to minister at Dr. Cho's church. As I started to witness to the flight attendant, Quentin said to me, "Ken, it's my turn." I retorted, "No, you talked to the waitress in San Francisco."

He said, "Yes, but you got to lead her to Christ." I replied, "But you actually got her to that point, so now it's my turn."

The flight attendant said, "I don't understand all that is going on here, but are you arguing over who is going to talk to me?" In unison, we replied, "Yes, we are!" She added, "Wow! No

> *Don't go out to win the world, win the world as you go out.*

one has ever done that for me." She then continued, "I really need God and a lot of help."

It was so easy to lead her to Christ — all in five minutes. Lifestyle evangelism should be fun, not something you dread to do. *Make life a mission — not an inter-mission.*

> *A real winner feels the gold medal hanging on his/her neck before the race starts.*

D.L. Moody said "Lord, I'm a leaky vessel, so I need to stay under the tap."

Endnotes

1 Gil and Corrinne Keith, *Personal Promise Bible* (Richland, WA: Phronesis International).

2 Joseph C Aldrich, *Lifestyle Evangelism* (Sisters, OR: Multonomah Press).

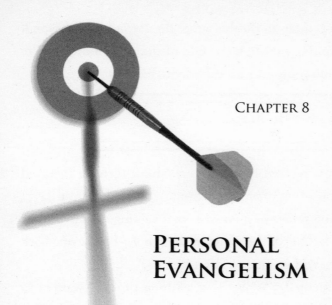

PERSONAL EVANGELISM

I minister every week in some of the world's greatest churches. Most of these pastors have a passion for the lost and teach "EVERYONE WIN ONE." Most don't just teach personal evangelism, they take one person at a time with them on the spot to watch how to win someone. It catches on as that person learns what to do and acquires the same vision and passion burning in his or her heart.

I don't think I'm the best soul winner in the world, but when I see opportunities, Jesus in me always takes over.

One pastor I know takes someone out to learn several times, then gets that person to teach someone else while he repeats the process with yet another. Soon 2 become 4, 4 are 8, 8 become 16. If you have a church of 1,000 and everyone wins just one, at the end of the first month you'll have 2,000.

If you teach these to do the same, the second month you'll double again to 4,000. At the end of the third month, there will be 8,000. This goes on exponentially.

> *Possibilities are unlimited.*

Getting involved is what it's all about (getting involved without appearing to be nosy or rude). On a plane one day, I was standing near two men who were talking. I smiled, they smiled back. One of them said to the other, "I just came back from Africa and was awake for 48 hours."

I commented, "Wow! That's a long time." I wanted to get involved.

His friend wanted to outdo him and said, "That's nothing, I was awake once for 59 hours."

I again commented, "That's *really* a long time."

Then he asked me, "What's the longest you were ever awake?"

I answered, "I was awake once for 17 days!" Each one of them questioned me, "Man, how did you do that?"

I stated, "I slept nights." Needless to say, everyone roared with laughter. Another chance to witness.

Think about the *Titanic*. People were content, even when they hit the iceberg. They were sure that

> *Paul Getty said that "in times of fast changes, it's our experience that becomes our worst enemy."*

even God couldn't sink this boat. They made a big mistake and were comfortable where they were until it was too late.

No change will always make everybody happy. I often think about those who laughed at the Wright Brothers as I am on an airplane, five miles up in the air, flying over 500 miles an hour. They wouldn't have believed it.

Jesus believed in change, and He changed the world. Jesus' ministry was in the marketplace and by the seashore, not just in the temple.

We have to warn people while there is time (Ezek. 33:6). The destiny of peoples' souls hangs in the balance. Witnessing and warning is not something easily done. But it's an assignment from Jesus that carries no options.

I believe that some Christians need a little more God-given *ego*.

You ask me what I'm saying. I know that *ego* is the Greek for *self* or *flesh*. It is not my intention to promote self, simply to say that since God esteems us, we need to esteem ourselves as His children and learn to appreciate the abilities He has given us.

> *Face the devil head-on with God-given authority.*

I'm saying to stop being so timid and letting the devil beat you up and run you down. Don't let the devil run all over you, convincing you that you can't do it. You are special, #1, a one of a kind, unique, wonderful and you're God's creation. He doesn't make junk. Wake up. Lift up your head. Take a risk.

Remember the story of David and Goliath. First of all, David had nobody voting for him. No one, including his family, really believed in him. He sure didn't look like a warrior or a leader. He spent his time tending the sheep, so he probably didn't smell too great either.

When Samuel came to anoint one of Jesse's sons to be Israel's next leader, David's seven brothers were called in. *He was totally rejected by his family.*

His brothers' qualifications were based on outward appearance. David was a man after God's own heart, and his heart was right. Even though David was always ready for battle, he wasn't drafted into the army like his brothers. They even got mad when he brought them food. *This teenager again was slighted.*

When this no-count shepherd boy heard the giant challenging God's people, his God-given ego took over. The giant's booming voice put fear and terror in the hearts and minds of the army. David was calm, confident, and ready. David's response was, "Who does this guy think he is, that he defies the living God's army?"

Everyone heard his seemingly boastful words. King Saul called for him. Saul was probably looking forward to meeting a giant of a man, tough and hard, standing before him. Was King Saul in for a surprise when this tender, teenage shepherd boy was ushered in!

David's confidence was evident as he told the king, "Don't let anybody be afraid of this guy, I will take care of him."

Saul answered, "You're just a kid, and the giant has years of training and fighting wars under his belt."

David refused again to let rejection put him down. He responded, "I'm a shepherd. A lion and a bear tried to steal one of my sheep. I went after them, killed them, and got my sheep back! I will slay this guy *with God's help.*"

King Saul did not see the winner material in this teen-aged shepherd boy. Wanting to protect David, the king put his big armor and helmet on him. I can see David unable to move in that big, heavyweight outfit.

David did not let this hinder him, destroy his potential, or mess with his mind. HE JUST COULDN'T DO IT SAUL'S WAY. He took it all off and said, "Thanks anyhow. I've never tried these. I HAVE TO DO WHAT WORKS FOR ME. I have a slingshot and I'll pick up some rocks, and I'm good with this."

Saul gave him these words of encouragement: "You go, and God be with you."

As David went out to face the giant, he again was insulted, this time by the giant. Goliath couldn't believe his eyes. It really ticked him off. He asked, "What do you think I am? Can't you find someone better than this? I'll feed him to the birds!" Goliath's ego was based on himself.

Now the *God-given ego* came forth in David, and he said, "You are trusting in your size and training, but I am coming in the name of the Lord of hosts, the God of the armies of Israel that you are defying. Today the Lord will help me kill you so everyone will know there is a God in

Israel!" He also declared, "The battle belongs to the Lord" (1 Sam. 17).

To be successful, followers must have real leaders. David became a true leader for the people of God. He continued to grow in abilities as he stretched for God. The shepherd boy that God had anointed became the king of the nation of Israel as he overcame the insults and walked with God.

The moment David knocked Goliath down, the Israeli army had new hope, new vision, and new courage. David actually saved a nation.

He had to do what worked for him. Each of us has to do what works for us. Let's be on a genuine "Mission Possible" like David. *With all the rejection, he refused to be put down.*

CHAPTER 9

SPEAKING THE RIGHT LANGUAGE

Have you ever listened to some computer guys talking about a technical issue? Or tried to understand the conversation of a couple of teenagers? You recognize that at least some of the words are English, but you have no idea what is being said.

We Christians are often guilty of the same kind of thing. We have developed our own jargon — Christianese. We use recognizable words, but they convey a different meaning to us than they might convey to someone who has no affiliation with our particular church.

Here are a few examples: born again, saved, walking in the Spirit, under the Blood, last days, rapture, Second Coming, believe on, prayed through. This list could go on and on.

Jesus was the greatest teacher of all time. He had a unique way to approach any situation. He made people think. He often answered questions indirectly by using a parable to illustrate (Matt. 8:23–27). He also used nature as an example in order to teach a lesson.

He didn't tell us to get the essentials, fill out a test, fill in the blank, put the puzzle together, or meet with a committee. He used what was common — boats, nets, fish, children, trees, and money.

Instead of just telling the disciples about washing others feet, and how to do it and when and why, He simply knelt down like a servant and began to wash the disciples' feet. He could do all this without uttering a word. His followers understood (John 13:7). Not everyone else understood such a lesson.

I was preaching about our worth to God, and why He said we have value. I took a five-dollar bill from my pocket and had someone in the audience come to help me. I gave him the bill and told him to crumple it up. He did it. I told him to open it up and tell me what it was. He responded that it was a five-dollar bill.

I told him to crumple it again and then drop it on the floor and step on it. He did. I repeated my question. The answer remained the same — a five-dollar bill.

My point was that no matter how you abuse the bill, it retains the value of five dollars. Likewise, when the devil tries to put you down, no matter how much he crumples you or steps on you, your value to God remains the same.

In Hawaii, a man told me, "I'm drowning in my problems." My comment was that "I surf on mine." He understood that. You have to talk so people can understand.

> *You are somebody, and Satan is defeated in your life if you resist him.*

I'm sure you have heard this before — "We rarely learn anything from the successes in our life. We only learn from our failures."

When you witness to someone and feel you have failed, remember it takes an average of seven times of hearing the gospel before someone accepts Christ. Maybe your witness to them was only number three. Don't think of it as a failure.

If you were put on trial for being a Christian, would there be enough evidence to convict you? The same thought applies to being a soul winner — *is there enough evidence to convict you?*

Many times, non-believers' ears are deaf to what we say, but their eyes are open to our example. Don't say one thing and live another — that's being a hypocrite. The word *hypocrite* comes from the Greek, and means *to speak from under a mask*. In the ancient Greek theater, the actors wore masks so that their true identities were obscured.

> *Don't just invite people to church; develop a relationship.*

Some people live like the iceberg that the *Titanic* hit. Their visible lifestyle is only the tip of the iceberg; the rest is under water. Don't be counterfeit; be genuine and transparent, without a mask.

Let's have a healthy church and be giant killers, foolish enough to believe God. Don't use excuses. Make up new ways to touch lives.

Once a man came onto an airplane, using crutches and with his leg in a cast. Wanting to get involved, I asked, "What happened to you?" He said, "I fell off a 15-foot ladder and broke my leg in two places."

Just getting involved I said, "Wow, is it getting better?" He replied that is was. I told him, "That's good, I'll pray that it all gets back to normal." Then I followed up with, "I once fell off a 40-foot ladder." I had everyone's attention.

Someone asked, "Did you get hurt badly?" I replied that I didn't even have a scratch. My audience expressed unbelief, until I added, "I fell off the bottom step!" Another opportunity to witness appeared.

I got involved with two people who were having a conversation about cats. One commented that there was nothing worse than letting a cat out of the bag. I chimed in, "Oh, yes there is."

"What is that?" one man questioned me. I replied, "Putting that cat back in that bag." Everyone laughed, and I had a witnessing opportunity.

I asked a man on an airplane, "What do you do for a living?" He told me he was a heart specialist. I exclaimed, "That's what I am!"

He asked me where I practice. I replied, "I don't, I'm good." He laughed and I had another opportunity.

Sometimes on flights the attendant will bring alcohol and ask, "Care for a drink!" I reply, "No thanks, care for a prayer?"

The many times I've done things like this have always ended up with the conversation during the flight. Several times I have led someone to Christ.

Another time a man asked me what I did. I said I help people rewrite their biographies. This lead to a discussion, and, again, people find Christ.

In response to my question about his occupation, a man told me, "I am a broker." I commented, "Wouldn't it be better to be richer?" We laughed together. Then I witnessed to him. He said the term "broker" had taken on a new meaning.

Don't assume someone is a Christian and that everything is okay with him or her. Statistics tell us that 61 percent of even 5th and 6th graders are not sure of their relationship with Jesus Christ.

If your method of witnessing isn't working, maybe it's time to change the bait. You never change your principles, but sometimes you may need to change your methods if you want results. Get out of your rut.

We are also this way many times in our church services. Change is

> *Just knowing what is wrong and what is right is not enough.*

very important in your life. You can't continue to do the same things and expect different results.

We only see the tip of the iceberg. Let's take a risk, change what needs to be changed. Examine new ways to do things that relate to people and to today. Ask others with experience to help you.

I was teaching at Evangel Cathedral in Spartanburg, South Carolina, and a little girl said, "I like Ken Gaub, he's not just another boring preacher. He's like my pastor, Dr. Charles Gaulden."

Sometimes we speakers actually think we are teaching God's word. What the audience may be thinking is that "if God is as boring as this speaker, I'm not interested." That's another reason why people don't come back.

Sometimes in our churches, everything seems okay on the surface. However, attendance is down, crowds are not flocking in, so we are going to small groups. There is confusion, people are leaving, and discontent is growing. Some cover up the real problem by beginning another program. It's like putting a band-aid on a broken arm.

Small groups shouldn't be directed at just Christians encouraging each other. They should be aimed at reaching pre-Christians and bringing them to God and into the church.

Small groups should make a positive impact on the neighbors of the host homes. The neighbors often don't even know they exist. When you meet at someone's home, be sure you are considerate. Don't park in someone's assigned space or block a driveway. As a home-host, you might explain to your neighbors why several cars come to your place on a certain day. Use the opportunity to invite them to come and listen in and have tea or coffee with you.

> *Real effectiveness in witnessing requires the Holy Spirit to lead you so you use the right language for each person.*

Remember that Jesus commissioned us to be witnesses. He didn't ask us all to be lawyers. We don't have to be able to debate all the fine points of doctrine, only to tell what God has done for us individually.

Once, eating in a cafeteria, I found another new way to witness that works for me. The waiter followed with my tray as I was looking for a place to sit down. I saw a man sitting alone in a booth for four.

I said to him, "Sir, would you mind if I share the other side of the table with you? You don't have to talk, and I won't bother you. I eat alone a lot, and I want to sit with someone so it looks like I have friends."

He laughed and said, "Sit down." I prayed over my food and started eating. The man asked, "Where are you from?"

I said, "Oh, you don't have to talk."

He laughed, and also stated, "I've been eating alone for three months since my wife died of cancer."

I was at the right place at the right time with the right man and doing the right thing. We got acquainted, and 20 minutes later, for the first time in his life, this 77-year-old man gave his life to Christ.

Be sure you don't sound like a computer when you're witnessing. Have fun. Be real. Enjoy talking to people.

CHAPTER 10

WINNING SHY PEOPLE

Dealing with someone who is shy usually takes a bit of patience and gentleness. Being loud and confrontational and drawing unwelcome attention your way will probably have an extremely negative effect on the conversation.

Don't mistake shyness or quietness for lack of opinion or for lack of intelligence. This may not be the case. Quiet, shy people are often very well read, and have well-defined opinions on many things. They often lack confidence, but are not stupid.

Shy people often need a bit more time to consider issues before they are willing to make a decision. They can get left out of participation in a fast-moving conversation because they need to process things a little longer before they are willing to offer an opinion.

Don't try a high-pressure approach. Present Christ simply and logically.

> *Allow time for the Holy Spirit to do His work.*

If you press too hard, you may get the person to acquiesce; this probably does not really mean that he or she agrees. My wife tells me that in a "discussion," I can talk so fast and have so many things going at the same time, that she just gets confused and decides that it's not worth the effort to continue. After she has had time to think about the situation, her point of view has probably not changed. I only think I won.

You might need more than talking, you may need to wear Christ. I'm not talking about a T-shirt with *Jesus Saves* on the front. Put Jesus on like a garment, and let them see what a true Christian is.

Jesus had a discerning, loving, understanding heart. He reached out to the hurting. Ask God to guide you to say the right thing at the right time. You can't say the wrong thing to the right person or the right thing to the wrong person. To witness to someone shy, you will need a reliable, logical approach. Jesus relied upon His Heavenly Father. We have the Holy Spirit.

Mark records the incident of the paralyzed man whose friends let him down through the roof. Jesus saw their faith. He told the man that his sins were forgiven.

Some of the rabbis sat judging Jesus. "Who does He think He is? Only God can forgive sins!" was their reaction. Jesus rebuked them, then turned to the paralytic and said, "Just so you know I have power to forgive sins, get up, pick up your mat and go on your way."

The man did, and those around gave glory to God and said they had never seen anything like this before. The natural yielded to the supernatural.

Results occurred because Christ was present. You will also see results when Jesus is present in your life.

Maybe you say, "But I'm the shy one! I find that it's hard for me to talk to others."

It's difficult for a lot of people to strike up a conversation with total strangers or even to bring up spiritual things with those they know. This can be overcome.

Start with the clerk at the supermarket, or someone else standing in line. Make a comment about the weather or something on the magazine rack. Or just say "hello" to the child sitting in the cart. Practice several times and it will get easier.

Go on to more complicated or controversial things a little at a time. Try an off-hand (natural) comment about how good God is. Or a statement about something you're doing at church. When you integrate your spiritual life into your everyday life, it gets easier and more natural.

CHAPTER 11

WINNING
TOUGH PEOPLE

One of the continuing education firms conducts a seminar entitled "Dealing with Difficult People." The basic premise of the course is that everyone is difficult (or tough) to certain other people. In a real sense, there is a lot of truth to this. (See the Personality Chart in chapter 3.)

Someone who is difficult for me to deal with may be the very person that *you* find easy to talk and witness to and win to Christ. "Tough" people often show a prickly outside to hide a soft inside.

They may have been hurt at sometime in the past, so they are afraid to allow anyone to get close enough to hurt them again. Some of these hurts run so deep that the feigned tough attitude is a cover-up. It may be easier for some people to reject everyone than to take a chance on being hurt again.

Before God saved him, my father-in-law was not an easy man to deal with. He was tough. He didn't really care whether or not he made friends. If you wanted to talk to him, you had to go find where he was (mentally or emotionally) and meet him there. He would not come out of his shell to find you. He was often very difficult for me to deal with, because we didn't have many common interests.

However, after God got hold of him, his entire attitude changed. He was truly an example of what the term "born again" really means. He was no longer the same person.

Most everyone has a "hot button," an interest that they are passionate about. By finding what that interest is, you have a place to start. For men, that may be sports, or cars, or outdoor things like fishing or hunting. Some women also have these interests, besides the standard "feminine" pursuits of family, sewing, or crafts. Most people also are willing to talk about their job. The weather can always be a conversation starter.

Just before my dad's 90th birthday, he visited a man who had cancer. The man had been a tough customer all his life. Dad spent some time with him and was able to lead him to Christ. The next day, the man passed into eternity. What a thrill that in the last hours of his life, he was introduced to the One who would welcome him home.

It also thrilled me that Dad was still winning people at 90. He told me, "Don't ever think you're too old for God to use you. And don't ever think anyone is too tough to win to Christ."

WINNING TOTAL STRANGERS

Witnessing to a total stranger on an airplane is exciting to me. I sometimes have to begin my approach by helping them put their suitcase overhead, or get them a blanket or pillow, so I don't appear to be trying to invade their privacy. It takes practice do this tactfully and succeed. It was awkward at first.

Be sensitive to the needs of those around you. They may not be having a great day. Remember that some people may have already had a bad experience along this line.

I was once sitting in first class when a man walked through with a "Jesus" T-shirt on and a big Bible under his arm. He declared rudely, "You're all going to hell."

I answered boldly, "I'm not!"

He just walked on by.

The man in the seat next to me said, "I like your kind of religion already." I hadn't even witnessed to him yet. What a great open door.

Don't insult, trick, ambush, or embarrass people. I used to board airplanes and, trying to be friendly and open a witness avenue, I would state, "Hi, I'm Ken Gaub from Yakima, Washington." Comments went like "Wow," "Good for you," "I'm happy for you," and "Whoopty-do!" or "I never heard of Yakima."

I decided this approach wasn't working. Then I read John 1:6: "There was a man sent from God, whose name was John." I thought that I could adapt that and make it work for me. Most people don't care where I'm from, how many books I've written, how many miles I've flown, or how many countries I've been in. So I changed my whole strategy.

The next time I flew and a man sat down beside me, I said, "Hi! My name is Ken and I'm a man sent from God to speak into your life." He exclaimed "Awesome!" It opened an immediate door to witness. I've had people scream, cry, drop their belongings, and cover their faces.

People do care when you care.

I've led many people to Christ with this approach. Try it. Just say, "I'm a man (or woman) sent from God to speak into your life."

Once a woman was going to sit beside me on an airplane. I said, "Hi, my name is Ken. I'm a man sent from God to speak into your life on this flight." She screamed, dropped her bag, and covered her face. The flight attendant turned around and asked what happened.

A man across the aisle said, "He's a man from God!" What door openers.

Once, in the Atlanta airport, a man asked me, "Where is the exit?" I pointed it out, but added, "Remember when you go through there it's an entrance to somewhere else." He looked so seriously at me. I went on to say, "When you go through there, you don't disappear. Every exit is an entrance to some place else. It's like life — when you exit this life, you go to heaven or hell." On this occasion, I led the man to Christ.

In the Chicago airport, the gate area was crowded and almost every seat was taken. A man walked over to me, pointed at the vacant seat beside me and asked, "Is this seat saved?" I replied, "I don't even think it goes to church."

He laughed and asked, "What do you do for a living?" Several people were witnessed to through that incident, and I've used the approach many times.

Because I fly so many miles, I'm usually upgraded to first class. I was in first class with seven other people on United. Nothing was happening. That always bothers me. When people are doing nothing, how do they know when they are through? Since things were so quiet, I decided to do something.

They served us a nice breakfast. I asked the lady beside me, "Do you want to buy my yogurt?" She replied, "No, I have yogurt."

I asked the people behind me the same thing. They also declined. I turned in my seat and asked the couple across the aisle. They didn't want it either. I heard someone say, "Why is that man selling his yogurt?"

About that time the flight attendant came down the aisle. I asked her if she wanted to buy my yogurt. She replied that she had lots of yogurt so why was I trying to sell the yogurt.

I told her, "The orange juice container said 'drink for your health' so I drank it. On the yogurt container is stated 'sell before August 8,' so I'm trying to sell it. There are a couple weeks left, so I think we can do it."

Everyone laughed and someone asked what I do for a living. I replied that I was eating, but when I finished I would tell them. When the trays were cleared, I knelt on my seat and talked to all seven of the others who were with me in first class. They heard a witness like they had never heard before.

One of them was a Christian and he commented that he was going to start witnessing more. That time, I didn't lead anyone to Christ, but I gave all of them much to think about. Several of them even thanked me.

Don't be afraid to invent new ways that will fit your personality to win others to Christ.

CHAPTER 13

WINNING RELATIVES

Many times our relatives know all about us and sometimes it "ain't good." How can we expect to win them if we haven't gone out of our way to touch them with love? You say some of them aren't lovely. So what, you've got some "warts" that aren't very nice, either. Why not reach out to them, drop them a note. Find out when their birthday is and send them a card or call them on the phone. Invite them over to eat. Be transparent with them. They already know you aren't perfect. Be honest with them, be kind and let real love shine. We all know the Bible teaches love (1 Cor. 13).

Ideas for your relatives:

1. Do your best to portray Christ to them in the way you live.

2. Forget your own personal agenda. Show them love.

3. Avoid quarrels and confrontations.

4. Always remember that even though they're your relatives, they may be crushed and hurting people with shipwrecked lives. Don't bring up their problems, be kind and love them. If they ask you for prayer, either on the spot or later, respond that you will be glad to pray. If they don't ask, don't push.

5. Avoid being judgmental.

6. Give them a break. Be sensitive.

7. Show them some mercy, even if you don't think they deserve it.

Respond to any angry words with a sweet attitude and forgiveness. Forgiveness is extremely important. It takes a big person to say "I'm sorry," and it also takes grace to say "That's okay," and mean it.

Israelis and Arabs are both descendents of Abraham. They often refer to each other derisively as "cousin." Shortly after the treaty between Israel and Jordan was signed, along the northern border, a group of Israeli school children were visiting a park. This area had been closed off for many years because of the conflict, and had just been declared safe because of the treaty.

A Jordanian soldier who was still carrying a grudge, purposely shot into the group, killing several of the girls. The incident caused outrage all over the world.

The (late) king of Jordan, Hussein, crossed the border to visit the families. He didn't go in pride, as you would expect of a king, he covered his head with the kafiah (scarf) of a Bedouin peasant and knelt before the parents of each of the girls, expressing his sorrow and humbly begging for forgiveness for his people. You would never expect a king to beg for forgiveness from anyone, but he did. He even blessed them financially.

King Hussein was noted as a peacemaker. Some young Jordanian radicals threatened to kill one of his family members. One of them, less than 20 years old, was given a life sentence by the courts. In the prison where he was serving his sentence, a helicopter landed only eight months after he began serving his time.

His name was called, and he was taken to the helicopter. When he saw that King Hussein was in the copter, he feared for his life. He was told to get on board. As they flew away, the king asked the young man, "Where did you live before you tried to kill one of my family?" As he told him, he was sure this was the end, not only for himself, but possibly for his entire family.

The king spoke to the pilot, and the helicopter changed course. He said to the young man, "I was very upset that you threatened to kill one of my family members. It certainly was wrong. Even though I know you were with some other radicals, I'm sure you will never again attempt anything like this." The helicopter landed near the young man's house, the king shook his hand and said, "You're forgiven," and let him go.

King Hussein spoke at a news conference shortly after this incident, and said these words:

> *"If we want peace in the Middle East, Arabs have to learn something. We have to stop seeking revenge and start practicing forgiveness."*

We all need to learn to be forgiving, especially with our relatives. We all love our relatives. They are family. We want them all to go to heaven when this life is over. Let's simply love them with all their faults. You have faults of your own. *Never give up on anyone; miracles happen.*

In effective witnessing, you must realize it is not just sowing the seed, but knowing how, when, and where to sow it. Building relationships can plow the field so the seed can grow.

CHAPTER 14

WINNING RELIGIOUS PEOPLE

Many religious people think they are on the road to heaven. Some of these have a family, take a vacation, have children and/or grandchildren, and are the nicest neighbors you could ever want. Many of them even go to church, know the pastor, and put money in the offering. They are good people and God loves them. But hell will be full of good, very religious people.

I try to challenge people in a way that doesn't put them down. I never tear down someone else's (religious) house. Instead, I build a house beside his/her house with Jesus in it and make it so good he/she wants to move in. He/she will destroy his/her own house.

This precept can apply whether the person claims to be a Christian, or if he or she is Moslem, Buddhist, Jewish, or some obscure group that I may never have heard of. Courtesy and a loving spirit speak more about the love of God than sarcasm and rudeness.

Often, before we can win someone to Christ, we must first win him or her to ourselves. Only after the person respects us will they begin to listen to the message of Christ's love.

There are also some people who have a spirit of religion that is demonic. I'm not talking about them.

Sometimes I have a unique way in a church to give an invitation for the good people to accept Christ. I've had thousands of people turn to Christ with this approach. You would have to see me in action with this to understand the way it actually happens.

Many times when giving an invitation for good people to accept Christ, there are people who have been sitting in the congregation for years and have never made a commitment do so. Just because they attend church and seem okay, doesn't mean everything is all right. I'm using my personality to get this done.

At other times, I give the invitation for "bad" people first. It's the same for everyone, we have to build a relationship with them, and let our relationship to God be seen.

Some churches think people should follow without question, because that way they don't have to think. When a pastor does more than he thinks he can do, people will follow.

They say that only 46 percent of adults and 35 percent of youth state that the church makes them think. In the messages that we preach the statistics are as follows:

87 percent say their mind wanders during the message.

35 percent say most sermons are too long.

11 percent of women and **5 percent** of men state that the sermon is the major source of what they know about God.

12 percent say that they remember what was preached last week.

40 percent of most congregations forget what the pastor said within half an hour.

60 percent forget after a day.

90 percent forget after a week.

98 percent of pastors believe they are very gifted speakers, according to a recent poll, but only.

74 percent of the congregations believe their pastor is a gifted speaker.

95 percent of pastors never lead anyone to Christ one-on-one.

98 percent of Christians never lead anyone to Christ one-on-one.

We need anointed ears to hear what is being preached. The Holy Spirit does wonders for people with open hearts, even though it may not have been much of a message.

CHAPTER 15

WINNING KNOW-IT-ALLS

I once met a man who knew everything, traveled everywhere, was there before I was, stayed longer and did more, but he didn't even have a passport.

Smart alecks will often interrupt you while you're talking. They are ready to teach you something, even if they know nothing about the subject and they didn't hear a word you said. They know all the facts (they think). Some really do know a little about a lot of stuff. Atheists often fall into this class. They know why the Church is not perfect. They are usually very critical. If you do something right and good, they will still find a way to criticize you.

They may have a list of do's and don't's. They tear down rather than build up. They are usually sure that what the church or pastor is doing is surely wrong. If you listen for a while, you will be glad God didn't call them to pastor that church. Maybe God knew they didn't know it all. Even if they persecute you, so what? No matter what subject you bring up, they are the walking answer book.

Usually when I talk to someone who claims to be an atheist and thinks he knows everything, I ask three questions. I don't know the answers either, but it establishes the fact that they don't know everything. I like to have fun with this.

My questions can be like these:

> "If a vehicle was traveling at the speed of light and you turned the lights on, would they work?"
>
> "What do you call a male ladybug?"
>
> "How do you know when you're out of invisible ink?"

Usually they will admit "I don't know." Once that is established as a fact, then we can begin to converse about more serious matters.

Sometimes I use statistics to open the door for witnessing. I ask, "What do you think of the statistics in *USA Today* that 80 percent of Americans believe that Christ will return to this earth? Fourteen percent did not believe and 6 percent either did not know or had no comment?" I ask what group they're in.

Sometimes I ask, "If you died, why would God let you into heaven?" Some answer, "Because I'm a good person,"

"Because I don't sin," "I'm not wicked," "I take care of my family," "God would never send anyone to hell."

Then there are some who say, "Because I gave my life to Christ, and I worship Him." Right answer!

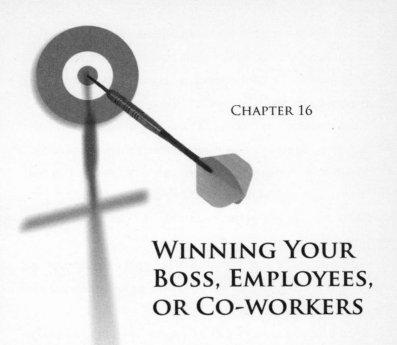

CHAPTER 16

WINNING YOUR BOSS, EMPLOYEES, OR CO-WORKERS

Because I am an employer, and all of my employees are already Christians, I admit that I don't have much first-hand knowledge of how things work in a large, mainly non-Christian office environment. However, some things just make common sense.

Be careful in the work place. Be sure your conduct will stand up under scrutiny. Treat your involvement in the workplace as a ministry.

People have a job to do; they are not at work for a lecture on salvation. You may have to stay within certain guidelines set down by management. During breaks, you may have an opportunity to witness. We hear reports of people using my *Wild*

Side video during lunchtime, since it contains a lot of humor. It has opened the door, and people have found Christ.

You have to look for opportunities. Sometimes you even have to make them. They won't jump out of a tree onto you.

Don't be confrontational. Tracts or some good Christian book may be effective. You might invite someone to attend a Christian movie with you, or some other event aimed at both entertainment and a gospel message.

With employees or subordinates, be careful of the appearance of coercion.

You cannot be a mediocre worker, showing up late and sneaking out early, and expect your boss to be impressed with your Christian testimony.

Don't be afraid to go out of your way to help someone. As a Christian, you need to be known for your "excellence on the job." You have to do more than look busy, you need to be productive.

If you're always running late, you should probably start sooner. I was standing in a bus and taxi area in New York City, waiting for a taxi. A bus started to pull away as a man came running up, hitting the side of the bus to get the driver to stop.

The driver kept on going, and the man, frustrated and out of breath came back to wait for the next bus. He said, "I guess I didn't run fast enough."

I retorted, "No, that wasn't the problem. You should have started sooner." He agreed.

It gave me an opportunity to witness.

You don't just decide your future, you decide your habits and they decide your future. In one sense, your passion decides your habits. Even in the workplace, you should not be without a passion to touch people's lives.

Be easy to work with, always ready to do a bit more than what is required (Matt 5:41). Have the reputation of being easy to get along with.

> *Promotions go to those who deserve them and have been consistently faithfully over a period of time. Remember that WINNERS do what LOSERS won't do.*

Be a team player for your company. Be on the building crew not the wrecking crew — build others up, don't try to tear them down.

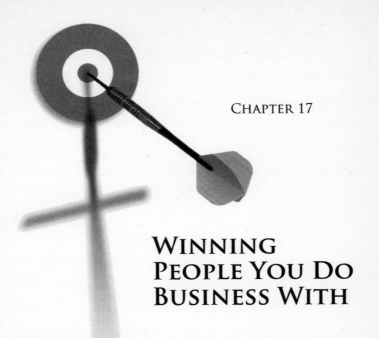

CHAPTER 17

WINNING PEOPLE YOU DO BUSINESS WITH

People's ears are often deaf to our words, but their eyes are open to our example. I believe you must have the following in order to be a real witness for Christ in the marketplace:

1. Credibility
2. Ethics
3. Integrity
4. Honesty

If you don't pay your local bills (on time), forget witnessing to your creditor. Identify and eliminate the "stuff" that might prevent you from having an effective testimony.

Keep commitments and appointments. Don't run away from your obligations. If things go haywire (and we know they will occasionally), call to apologize and reschedule, hopefully arriving a bit earlier than the appointment.

Be dependable. Don't get involved in "shady" deals. Be known as a "straight-shooter."

Remember that the people with whom you do business are prospects, not suspects. Don't waste an opportunity to thank them for a job well done, and show appreciation.

> *A person's greatest emotional need is to feel genuinely appreciated.*

When dining out, be sure to tip properly. Ten percent used to be the standard — now that is only sufficient in a diner or coffee shop. Fifteen percent is a minimum in a nice place — more if the service is great. If you don't tip properly, don't witness to your server, or tell him/her where you go to church. It will embarrass your pastor.

Be careful not to keep a waitperson from his/her duties while you try to witness. They are working. You can get a little word in here and there, but be sure to leave a good tip. You can't get into long discussions with them. They are there to serve you (and probably several other tables). They are not free from duties and just there for you to preach to them.

If you have a disagreement over service, or the quality of a product, take it to the management. It can't be corrected if the company is not aware that there is a problem. But always try to disagree agreeably.

There is an old saying that it's possible to "catch more flies with honey than with vinegar." While most of us aren't interested in catching flies, per se, the principle that you win more battles with kindness and politeness than by causing a scene does apply.

You don't need to let everyone "walk all over you" in order to "act like a Christian," but be careful of your attitude.

Be known for your friendliness.

Evangelism should be very exciting and full of love. My dog made it clear the first day I had her that she loved me, with licks and nuzzling close to me and tail wagging. That day, she became part of our family.

On cold nights, she knocks on the screen door with a foot, so we let her into the entryway where she lays on a carpet piece. She looks up at me with her tail wagging, saying thank you for being kind to me when it's so cold out there. After she gets warm, she stands up and lets us know she wants out. Everything is okay now.

Love will show, even with a dog. It certainly should show with others around us and especially the world.

CHAPTER 18

WINNING YOUR MATE

One of the biggest heartaches in life for a Christian can be living with an unsaved mate, not only because of the day-to-day difficulties, but also because of the knowledge that they are lost for eternity.

Start by treating your pre-Christian mate with kindness and respect. Be positive in your approach to him or her. You can win him/her without preaching, or continually nagging him/her to go to church. Be honest with your motives.

The apostle Peter advised wives to live lives that were so loving and circumspect that their husbands would believe in Christ because of them. This also applies the other way. Guys, let your life be so kind and Christ-like that she can't help but realize what a difference He has made in your life.

Ladies, be sure that you don't allow your church activities to impact negatively on your responsibilities at home. When you spend so much time at church that the house is a big mess, meals are non-existent, and laundry is stacked to the ceiling, your husband is not likely to think kindly of your "testimony."

Don't use manipulation as a tactic.

One woman who wanted to win her husband to Christ kept inviting Christian friends over to their home. Her main intention was soul winning. She laid tracts and Christian books all over the house. She even taped tracts to his razor, and stuffed them into his pockets. He got more and more defensive, and developed a great dislike of Christians, especially preachers — just because they were preachers.

She decided to have her pastor and his wife over for some gumbo (a kind of seafood soup) that she loved, but which her husband intensely disliked. After the meal had begun, she asked her pastor, "How do you like my gumbo?"

There was a moment of complete silence. While the husband waited, expecting a polite lie from the pastor, the wife continued, "Be honest, how do you like it?"

The pastor looked down momentarily, then gathered courage and told her, "Sister, I appreciate your work as a member of the church, but this is probably the worst gumbo I have ever tasted!"

She sat in stunned disbelief. Her husband nearly collapsed in laughter. "See," he chortled, "I've been telling you that for years! I finally found someone honest enough to agree with me."

A bond was formed between the husband and the pastor, and it was not long before he came to Christ.

One woman who continually nagged her husband about paying tithes heard me mention that if the husband is not a Christian, he is not under obligation to tithe. If he gives her undesignated money, she should pay tithe on that amount.

She apologized to her husband about nagging him to tithe. She told him she had heard me and realized that she was wrong. He came to church that Sunday night for the first time to hear me. I didn't mention tithe. He gave his life to Christ; now he tithes.

Winning a mate really boils down to love, understanding, tenderness, and patience. A pre-Christian husband was watching Sunday sports on TV. The last thing he wants to hear from his Christian wife as she returns from church is "Why won't you go to church with me?"

Instead, she should ask him, "How's the game going? Who's winning?" Then she might add, "Would you like a sandwich as you watch the game?"

There might even be times when she should skip church in order to have an outing with her husband. (I know that statement won't set well with some of you, but think about it.)

Bathe your relationship in constant prayer, asking God to make you a witness of the life-changing power of the gospel.

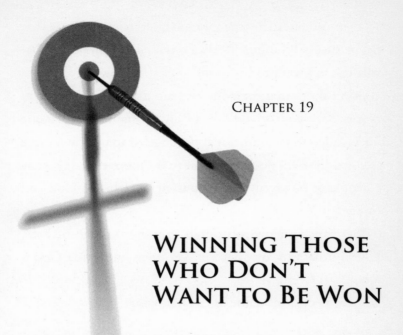

CHAPTER 19

WINNING THOSE WHO DON'T WANT TO BE WON

I believe that basically the world really wants to love God; it's *us* they don't like. To open a door for witnessing, I sometimes ask someone to help me with a personal survey. I might even add that I'm writing another book.

Here are some of the questions:

1. Do you attend church?
2. Is the church exciting to you?
3. Are you a member of a church?
4. When were you born again?
5. Do you have daily devotions with your family?
6. Do you really believe you have an ongoing relationship with Jesus? When did it start?

It's important to love people and build relationships. That can't be stressed too much. Always remember, the world basically doesn't want to be "won."

Don't think that someone else can do it better than you can. Yes, I know that God called Billy Graham. But each one of us is called to be a missionary/evangelist to our own piece of the world. God does need you to do more than just pray for people to be saved. Make yourself available to God and to others.

There are so many in trouble, groping through divorce, financial situations, or whatever. Let them know that God is their answer (Matt. 6:33).

I hear people say some of the following:

1. The world doesn't want to be won.

2. Someone can do it better than I can.

3. Besides that, I'm not a missionary evangelist. If they want to be won, the Lord will work it out, why does He need me?

4. I'll pray for them. Didn't Jesus say that they wouldn't "come to me to receive eternal life"?

5. Those in trouble, groping through life's problems need someone to share Jesus with them.

6. God will never send anyone to hell.

Be the kind of person who makes them change their minds. Do what you can to reach them. It's your job (and mine) to win others and *God needs you* to do more than pray.

CHAPTER 20

SOME DON'TS

Peorle will listen to you if they feel you really care for them.

DON'T tell people they can't be happy without Jesus. Many are happy in ways we don't know about. Some people are extremely happy with the possessions they have, the money they are making, and where they are going. They love their family and their lives.

DON'T have a canned "sales pitch" that you give everyone, like a used car salesman trying to sell a sports car to a 90-year-old woman.

Everyone has individual needs. Jesus treated people like individuals. He met them where they were, and focused on the person, not using the same method for everyone. Paul said he became "all things to all men" in order to reach some.

Some professing Christians look bad to the non-believer. They fight, they gossip, run everyone down, and can't get along with one another. Their heads are full but their hearts are empty. Although they are witnessing, their message isn't ringing true.

Let me tell you a personal story.

I was about 22, and getting on an airplane for the first time. I'm out to win the world. I know they will listen to *me*. I then believed I was really the best there was at winning people to Christ. Was I in for a real surprise and a rude awakening!

I was sitting next to a woman, and I had an odd feeling sitting beside her. She didn't speak to me, so I was waiting for a chance to witness. Time went on. About 30 minutes in the air, they served us a "meal." *Now here is my chance!* I thought. I'll pray out loud over my food so she can hear me, too. Maybe this will open the door. So I did.

Then I noticed she also bowed her head and seemed to quietly pray.

When she finished, I asked, "Are you a Christian?"

Her answer really unnerved me. She said, "No, I'm a witch!"

In my sheltered life, I had never encountered anything like this! I blurted, "A real witch?" She answered affirmatively that witches were all real.

I felt cold chills go up my back. Then she added (to make things worse for me), "I know you prayed to God over your food. I prayed to Satan over mine." I couldn't believe what I was hearing, so now I'm going in for the final blow. I will show her that she's wrong and that I'm right, and she needs Christ.

Then, without thinking, I blurted out, "If you're a real witch, why are you on this plane? How come you're not riding your broom?"

You don't really want to know the rest of this story. It is sufficient to say, everything was downhill after that. She was not won to Christ, and I didn't make a good impression for Christ, either. However, I learned what *not to do* — a tough lesson for me.

We have to start thinking daily about what we can change to help touch more people with the gospel.

The other day a man told me he called a certain church on Saturday because he needed prayer right away. The answering machine informed him that no one was available until nine on Monday morning. Some churches have emergency numbers on their answering message where someone with a real need can call 24/7. This might be something all churches could consider.

You have to not only know what to do, how to do it, and where and when to do it, but what *not* to do.

CHAPTER 21

THE FOLLOW-UP

There is more to salvation than just saying the sinner's prayer. That is just the start. Jesus made disciples, and commissioned us to do the same. Effective leadership makes great, aggressive disciples.

Follow-up is so neglected in many churches. During Jesus' final days He spent extra time with those He loved (Luke 10:38–42).

Jesus often took time with individuals. After the conversion of the Samaritan woman, He stayed two extra days, and many more believed in Him (John 4:39–40). He also took time to visit Zaccheus in his home (Luke 19).

Frequently, Jesus would take His disciples with Him in a retreat to some mountainous area of the country where He was relatively unknown, seeking to avoid publicity as far as possible. They took trips together to Tyre and Sidon to the northwest (Mark 7:24), to the "borders of Decapolis" (Mark 7:31), and "the parts of Dalmanutha" to the southeast of Galilee (Mark 8:10) and to the "villages of Caesarea Philippi" to the northeast (Mark 8:27).

These journeys were made partly because of the opposition of the Pharisees and the hostility of Herod, but primarily because Jesus felt the need to get alone with His disciples.

On a hill in Galilee, Jesus gave to the church a strategic way to win the world (Matt. 28:18–20). Winning people to Christ is not optional for the dedicated Christian.

Jesus believed in follow-up. He even checked on how they were doing (Mark 6:30). The disciples faced many challenges. Jesus never let them stop, whether they had failures or successes.

In some of the world's greatest churches, pastors are reporting to me after I've spoken there about great results in winning people one-on-one. Even new, dedicated, tithe-paying Christians are using some ideas I have given them to win people to Christ.

We don't turn newborn babies loose and expect them to survive without attention. Likewise, newborn baby Christians need nurture so that they can grow and become mature believers and workers in His kingdom.

CHAPTER 22

FINAL NOTES

God wants us to have a servant's heart. We should be not only teachable, but also sensitive to the needs of others. If you see the big picture, and want to bear fruit for Christ, you will also see new opportunities and cultivate ways to make things happen.

Your purpose and thinking should be unbeatable; your confidence in God should be firm. You should daily portray a "never give up" spirit. You will inspire others to follow you as you follow Christ.

You shouldn't have to prove anything, but you should have a passion to win the lost.

If you make a mistake (and don't we all), admit it, use it as a steppingstone, and move on.

> *If you think you're a leader, but no one is following you, you're probably just out for a walk.*

You might consider these three things, when you goof:

1. You anticipated incorrectly.

2. You planned poorly.

3. You missed key factors because you focused on secondary issues.

We need a positive, victorious, happy life. Lifting up Jesus, praising Him, thanking God, and obeying Him.

Allow me to paraphrase the 28th chapter of the Book of Deuteronomy:

> And this will happen, if you listen carefully to the words of God and do the things you know to do, God will lift you up: and blessings will come to you, blessings will run after you, if you obey the words of God.
>
> You will be blessed in the city, and out in the country. Your children will be blessed. Your business will be blessed. You will have plenty. You will be blessed when you go out and when you come home. The LORD will fight your battles, and your enemies will run away. God will open His good treasure for you. God will make you the head, not the tail. You will lend and not borrow. All this if you pay attention to the words of God.

Verses 1–14 list about 30 blessings that will actually run after you and catch you if you obey Him.

Verses 15–68 list about 120 curses for disobedience to God. Nothing you do will be blessed; everything will be cursed — your life, your health, your finances. Your enemies will get the best of you. Your children will be cursed. Nothing will work out like you want it to.

I don't know about you, but I don't want curses coming after me. I want all the blessings I can get. So I intend to obey God. I also plan to introduce as many people as I can to the Savior, so that they can share in His blessings.

Here are some "Rules for Success":

1. Be prompt in greeting people (Hello — Good Morning, etc.).

2. Greet people by name if possible. (People love their names.)

3. Compliment at least three people every day.

4. Treat everyone as you want to be treated. We get back what we give out, so be generous.

5. Always tell the truth — honesty and integrity are necessary.

6. Keep your promises.

7. Be on time for appointments (even if it costs you).

8. Be known as a friendly, positive person (on the phone, too).

9. Always leave things better than you found them.

10. Remember that *winners* do what *losers* won't do.

11. Live beneath your means.

12. Don't judge a day by its weather.

13. The best things in life aren't things.

14. Be tough-minded, but tenderhearted; be kinder than you have to be.

15. Learn to be cheerful, even when you're not happy.

16. Don't waste an opportunity to tell someone you appreciate him or her.

17. Don't rain on the other guy's parade.

18. Don't tear down a fence until you find out what is on the other side.

19. Remember that *overnight success* usually takes several years.

For more information about Ken's schedule,
speaking engagements, and ministry:

Ken Gaub Worldwide Ministries
P.O. Box 1
Yakima, WA 98907

1-800-536-4282

Other books by Ken Gaub

ANSWERS TO QUESTIONS YOU'VE ALWAYS WANTED TO ASK

Christian humorist Ken Gaub provides answers to over 50 topics: Why can't Christians agree on doctrine? Do the redeemed still have to obey God? Why does a good God allow evil to exist? Are Christians promised wealth?

ISBN: 0-89221-207-1 • 144 pages • $9.99 ($15.99 Can.)

DREAMS, PLANS, GOALS

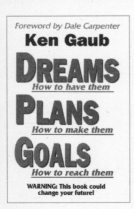

Discover practical ways to turn your dreams into reality, make your plans succeed, and set goals and achieve them. Ken Gaub travels the country motivating Christians to make a positive difference in their world.

ISBN: 0-89221-244-6 • 144 pages • $9.99 ($14.50 Can.)

Available at Christian bookstores nationwide

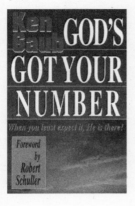